Let the Rivers Flow

"Perhaps you have attended a family gathering—perhaps even a family reunion. First, there might have been greetings and expressions of love towards the host and often followed by an exciting time of sharing good news and exciting stories. Later a sumptuous meal might be provided by the host. Still later the host bids the guests farewell, often with a parting gift or blessing.

The *open meeting* concept described herein by Lori Byers often follows the pattern of the family gathering—but in this case the family is God's family.

The *open meeting* begins by greeting the Father and offering to Him gifts of worship and praise. Then follows a time during which good news and exciting stories are related in order to ascribe honour and glory to Father God and to build up and encourage brothers and sisters in the Lord. Later, it is often the case at a family reunion, everyone gets to enjoy a feast provided by an earthly father or beloved host. So also are participants in an *open meeting* afforded a feast of teaching from the Word of God. Well-nourished from the Word of God, our Father also responds to the needs of His followers. Participants in an open meeting may—before returning to their homes—participate in, or receive, prayer for their needs and for the needs of others.

Based on her years of ministry experience, Lori Byers has addressed many of the issues involved in *open meetings* and she has done so in a very forthright and compassionate manner. The instructional material contained herein will certainly be of great benefit to any who seek to break traditional models of ministry in order to more fully embrace people and their needs.

Through her ground-breaking work in the area of *open ministry*, Lori Byers has opened the door to successful ministry which involves all of the people during the entire *open meeting*.

Thank you Lori for your insights into this important area of ministry. Your model of *open ministry* has touched many people, and will yet touch, many more. Congratulations on a work well done!"

Warren E. Hathaway, Ph.D

"Awesome! This book was a long time coming. I got saved under New Testament Outreach Ministries Int. almost 13 years ago when Pastor Lori and her team brought the Gospel Tent to Kawacatoose, SK. 27 of us got saved; we had no church and no preacher. When the meetings were over, Pastor Lori continued to minister us by phone in those early days. *"Let The Rivers Flow"* would have been a tremendous help to us. I know from our experience that this is going to be an awesome hand book for the ones who are looking to have open meetings. We are proof that the scriptural instructions in this book work. We have been taught this by Pastor Lori and carried on in this style. We have awesome church services with the Spirit of God moving, the ministry of God's Word and the joy of seeing believers raised up and used by God in our meetings. I know Pastor Lori and the love she has for Jesus and people. This book truly is a God-send. It is my prayer that people who need to know what to do to have open meetings be drawn to this book and be truly blessed with it."

Pastor Marcy Rosling

Kawacatoose Light House Ministries

Let the Rivers Flow

Rev. M.L.(Lori) Byers

Copyright © 2014 M.L. (Lori) Byers

All rights reserved.

For permission to copy for individual and/or group Bible Study purposes, please contact author at:
ntomi.l.d@gmail.com

All scripture quotations are from the King James Version of the Holy Bible unless otherwise stated.

Scripture quotations marked NLT are taken from the Holy Bible, New Living Translation, copyright © 1966, 2004. 2007 by Tyndale House Foundation. Used by permission of Tyndale House Publisher, Inc., Carol Stream Illinois 60188. All rights reserved.

Scripture quotations taken from AMPLIFIED BIBLE, Copyright © 1954, 1958, 1962, 1965, 1987 by the Lockman Foundation. All rights reserved. Used by permission. (www.Lockman.org)

ISBN: 978-1-77354-154-9

Library and Archives Canada catalogue ...
1. Open Meetings
2. Body Ministry
3. House Churches

Publication assistance and digital printing in Canada by

PUBLISHING
PageMaster.ca

Dedicated to the Glory of God and with love to:

Phil and Mildred Tretwold
&
Don and Millie Ross
who had the courage to believe
and who paved the way
with God led example, exhortation and
encouragement.

Thank You!

This book is also prayerfully dedicated
to all those within whose hearts God has
placed the desire to "let the rivers flow"
as you meet together in Jesus Name.

May God truly bless you and
use you for His glory!

Contents

In Appreciation 1

Introduction 3

1 Treasures in Earthen Vessels 5

2 Open Meetings: Beginning A Group 10

3 Prayer And Unity 12

4 Entering Into The Presence Of God 20

5 The Moving Of God's Spirit 29

6 Open Sharing And Body Ministry 35

7 Teaching And Preaching God's Word 41

8 Special Prayer For Salvation, Healing And Other Needs 49

9 Why We Meet Together 54

10 Determining Where And When To Meet 59

11 Twenty-Four/Seven Christianity 62

12 Meeting Together As A Body Of Believers 64

13 Open Sharing: Purpose And Guidelines 67

14 Dealing With Issues Of Correction 70

15 We Are Called To Believe God: Not To Limit God 77

16 Expanding Vision For Kingdom Purposes 84

17 Godly Leadership 89

18 Finances And Integrity 97

19 Preparing For Good Meetings 101

Conclusion 113

   Foot Notes and Credits 115

   Appendix A 116

IN APPRECIATION

First and foremost, I want to thank the Lord for His goodness, His mercy, His love and for all He has done in my life. I also want to thank Him for Phil and Mildred Tretwold, Don and Millie Ross and others, who during years of life-changing ministry, have encouraged and taught God's people to come forth in the call of God through open meetings and body ministry. Fruit remains, as many who learned to minister in those meetings are in ministry today and are also teaching others to do the same.

I also thank God for Dorothy Carbert, my friend and co-labourer in the Gospel. Since 1994 we have held open meetings together and we praise God for each person who has been touched by Him and who is coming forth in the call of God. Thank you Dorothy for all your support, prayers encouragement and typing as this book has been in progress and now is finally written. I thank God for you and for your friendship.

I thank the Lord for Jane Martin, who along with her husband Larry, traveled many miles with the NTOMI Team. Thank you Jane for your willing heart and for your care in the initial editing of this book.

I also thank the Lord for Velma White, who worked together in the Gospel with Dorothy and I from 2000 - 2016. I have appreciated your willingness and all the typing which was done to finalize the first manuscript. Thank you Velma for your hard work and encouragement regarding this book.

Along life's journey, God has some wonderful surprises. Just as the 2018 revision of *'Let The Rivers Flow'* began, Laura Geelen came north to minister and undertook the editing of the revised edition. Then, despite their busy schedules; Dorothy Carbert and Sharon Williams offered to retype the manuscript. Thank you Laura and thank you Dorothy and Sharon. Your gifts of time, and your labour of love is so appreciated.

Without a team, little is accomplished. I also thank the Lord for the NTOMI Team and the Body of Christ. Together, may we His people see the increasing ongoing manifestation of God's presence and His visitation, as we glorify Him and *"Let The Rivers Flow"*.

INTRODUCTION

There is a hunger for more of God in the hearts of many of His people today. This is evidenced by their expressed longing for greater liberty and freedom of the moving of the Holy Spirit in their midst. Some believers, such as those in a number of our northern villages in Canada, have no evangelical church, gathering place, or pastor and have held little hope of this changing in the near future. They have shared how they have felt like a forgotten people and have so longed for true fellowship with believers and teaching about the things of God. Other believers have not found the freedom they are longing for in the traditional church of their area. There are yet others, who represent the traditional church, who are looking for a way to have more open meetings and have themselves expressed a longing to experience this type of freedom.

It is for these precious hungry children of God that this handbook[1] has been written. It is my prayer that numerous readers will lay hold of the scriptural principles addressed in this book and that it will be a blessing and

---

1   It is important to note that at any time in this book, when the Spirit of the Lord is cited, that it implies the Spirit will always agree with the Word as 1 John 5:8 has recorded in the Scriptures.

encouragement for those who long to let the river of God flow afresh, in and through His people, as they meet together in Jesus' Name.

ONE

TREASURES IN EARTHEN VESSELS

There are many types of meetings such as prayer meetings, bible studies, discussion groups, open meetings as well as "traditional" Sunday church meetings, which are participated in by God's children. The focus of this handbook is on open meetings which includes body ministry: defined as a scriptural sharing from the body of believers in attendance at the meeting. In this type of meeting the order, content and duration of the meeting are not usually prearranged. The group, as well as the leader in charge, endeavour throughout the meeting to be led by the Holy Spirit in terms of who will minister at any given time. Group participation is encouraged and open sharing is valued as the different participants seek to give what the Lord has laid on their hearts under the direction and anointing of the Holy Spirit.

I was twenty years old when I first experienced open meetings. At that time God led me into fellowship with a group of believers who met in a hall in Calgary. They were on fire for the Lord and loved Jesus with all their hearts. Church was not simply a building we went to on

Sunday — we were the Church. Christianity was a way of life, 24/7, not just something we "did." We learned to seek God with all our hearts. When we gathered together, it was exciting! We never knew what God was going to do or who He was going to use. We could hardly wait!

I remember God moving in awesome ways. The praise and worship was incredible. Many times people would play instruments in the Spirit, prophetic songs would come forth and we would dance before the Lord with all our might as the holy, awesome presence of the Lord would come into our midst. Sometimes the Song of the Lord would go on for hours. As the Holy Spirit moved and touched hearts and lives, the words and music of the song were spontaneously given by the Lord. While individuals yielded to the leading of the Lord, the song was directed and led by the Holy Spirit. Prophetic songs would come and the Song of the Bride and the Bridegroom was freely heard (spontaneous Spirit-given and Spirit-led songs in which Christ, as the Heavenly Bridegroom, and the Church, as His prospective Bride sing responsively to each other as God moves prophetically through different people). Sometimes those in passing vehicles would come and roll down their windows as they stayed to listen to the beauty of what they were hearing. The people walking by on the streets would be touched by the power of God as the Song of the Lord was sung by His people.

I also remember how we all sought God on Saturdays for Him to move in and through His people in the Sunday's services. Most of us (especially the young people) spent the day in fasting and prayer. We did not do this because we "had to"; we wanted to! We wanted to be ready for Sunday and to be prepared for what God would do, whether in us or through us, as He moved by His Spirit. None of us wanted to miss out either on what God was doing or what He was about to do!

I remember a nine year old boy getting up to read a scripture in the Sunday service. As the anointing came upon him, he began to exhort and then to prophesy the Word of the Lord like a prophet of old. The gifts of the Spirit flowed freely in those meetings and God used young and old alike, to preach, to pray and to prophesy. People were thrilled as different ones came forth in God. Most of the young people from that church (including myself) are in full-time ministry today. God called us, taught us, established us in the Word and brought us forth on our knees. We were birthed in the fire and anointed to go forth and minister in Jesus' Name.

I thank God for the time He had me at the hall in Calgary and for the privilege of being in that assembly. I also thank the Lord for the atmosphere of godly love and the desire for God that permeated my early days there. People opened their hearts and their homes. Instead of superficial conversation, hours — wonderful life-giving hours — were given to talking about the Lord. He and He only was the center of our lives, and time and time again we would see this modeled by the other believers we fellowshipped with within the assembly.

I thank Him for those leaders who trusted God enough to let the young come forth, and who were not afraid to let God have His way in the services. They had the courage to put their trust in God and to fight the "fight of faith" for the will of God, rather than man's will, or the enemy's will, to come forth in the meetings and in the peoples' lives. They endeavored to maintain, by the Holy Spirit, God's order in the services. This was never an easy task, but how much better is the freedom of God rather than the bondage of man and, once that freedom is tasted, how difficult it is to live without it!

Although we are imperfect vessels, there is a treasure in each of His children which will come forth in the freedom of the Holy Spirit as God is allowed to move in and through His Body. As this happens, His glory begins to come forth and the life of the Spirit of God is ministered to and through His people,

> *We have this treasure in earthen vessels, that the excellency of the power may be of God and not of us.*
> *–2 Corinthians 4:7*

Lives are changed for time and eternity when God's purposes, rather than the purposes of men, are accomplished. May God truly have His way in each of us!

For many years now God has led our ministry to have open meetings. We have personally found that these types of meetings have been blessed of God whether they have been held in homes, in churches, in rented buildings or in our gospel tent which we travel with during the summer. It has been a real joy to minister to and to receive from God's many-membered body. It is wonderful to see Him raising up ministries as His people become rooted and grounded in Him, setting themselves apart to seek Him, and committing themselves to become all He has called them to be.

We have been asked to share some of what we have learned along the way. Although volumes could be written about open meetings, at this time we have felt led to develop somewhat of an overview or handbook. As each group seeks the Lord, He Himself will lead and will bring forth the leaders, the people and the meetings as He wills. He alone is the expert in this, He delights to reveal Himself and His ways to those who hunger and thirst after Him.

TWO

OPEN MEETINGS: BEGINNING A GROUP

In order to have an open meeting, there must first be those who desire to have one. This can happen in several ways. Sometimes God places the desire for open meetings in the hearts of a group of people who have been together in other types of meetings. At other times God will place in the heart of just one or two people the desire to begin an open meeting. In other cases open meetings start as the gospel touches lives in communities where there are no churches. The people begin meeting together for fellowship and worship and to study the Word and often times a church is birthed through this.

When this desire for open meetings comes from God's leading, it grows in peoples' hearts as they delight themselves in the Lord. As they commit their way unto the Lord, trusting in Him, He begins to bring it pass (Psalm 37:4-5). God begins to give His direction, strategies and timing for the meeting. As people look to Him and as each walks in obedience to Him, God's plan for them begins to unfold. To truly wait on God for His direction and then to walk in obedience to it, are both of paramount importance. What God initiates He will bless. He has promised that the "willing and obedient shall eat the good of the land" (Isaiah 1:19).

As people wait upon the Lord in prayer, God will begin to confirm the leadership of the group and to answer practical concerns, such as where and when to meet. He also will begin to move in the hearts of those He would have to come. Dependence on God and obedience to God each step of the way is vital, for Jesus said:

> *I am the vine, ye are the branches: He that abideth in me, and I in him, the same bringeth forth much fruit: for without me ye can do nothing.*
>
> *–John 15:5*

It is true — without Him we can do nothing. If we want what we do to count for time and eternity, it must be done by His Spirit working through us.

This attitude of utter dependence upon God and obedience to God must continue on as the meetings become a reality. Only in this way will we see the Spirit of God continue to come and to move as only He can.

THREE

PRAYER AND UNITY

There is a remnant of God's people who hunger and thirst after God's righteousness and they will be filled.

> *Blessed are they which do hunger and thirst after righteousness: for they shall be filled.*
> *—Matthew 5:6*

This people will be empowered by the Holy Ghost and will be strong and do exploits for the kingdom of God.

> *But ye shall receive power, after that the Holy Ghost is come upon you: and ye shall be witnesses unto me both in Jerusalem, and in all Judaea, and in Samaria, and unto the uttermost part of the earth.*
> *—Acts 1:8*

> *…The people that do know their God will be strong and do exploits .*
> *—Daniel 11:32b*

As they rise up in the Lord, this people will walk together in His glory. The blessing of God will be upon them as they spend time in prayer and walk in unity. People will be drawn to the presence of God which is upon those that God is raising up.

> *...Arise, shine; for thy light is come, and the glory of the LORD is risen upon thee.*
> *For, behold, the darkness shall cover the earth, and gross darkness the people: but the LORD shall arise upon thee, and his glory shall be seen upon thee.*
> —Isaiah 60:1-2

The Scriptures show the local assembly as a place believers are to be raised up to come forth in ministry (Ephesians 4:7-16). Participation in open meetings can be a powerful means of seeing this accomplished as people learn to hear from God and minster that which God gives them to minister.

The success of open meetings is, first and foremost, a function of prayer and unity with God's plans and purposes.

PRAYER

The key to a good meeting is a meeting birthed in prayer. It is important that each person be taught and encouraged to spend time in prayer in preparation for each meeting. The responsibility of open meetings does not rest on the leader alone, but upon the whole body of believers — whether they are young or old in age or in the Lord. As each one prays, God will begin to announce His plan and cause it to manifest.

> *Call unto me, and I will answer thee, and shew thee great and mighty things, which thou knowest not.*
>
> *–Jeremiah 33:3*

We serve the God who answers prayer! God will often begin to give His plan and His direction for the meeting as we pray. Oftentimes, we have seen God give specific scriptures or songs, as well as the message for the meeting. At other times, He will speak through a scriptural dream or a vision and begin to show what He desires for the meeting.

As people pray, God also at times will give warnings ahead of time regarding the meetings. God gave such a dream to one the ladies in our Slave Lake assembly regarding two psychics. They later came into our meeting and wanted to "minister and prophesy" over the people. She recognized them as soon as they walked in the door. God also spoke to several of us — some ahead of time, and others at the meeting as the psychics walked in. Because the people knew by the Holy Spirit what was going on, the psychics could not have their way, even though it was an open meeting. When they tried, everyone quietly prayed and the psychics ended up getting irritated and angry. They could not function in the meeting. One of them actually said in frustration, "I can't do anything here." It was true, and we praise God for this. I believe it was because people were seeking God to have *His* way in *His* meeting. God looks after His people as they seek Him and put their trust in Him.

As we seek God in prayer, He also prepares us, cleanses our hearts and empowers us to hear and to obey Him during the meeting. People have testified how God has cleansed their hearts from things like fear, intimidation, pride, competition and jealousy while in prayer. This is so important, for these are the very things that hinder the moving of God's Spirit and bring forth death rather than life amongst God's people.

How wonderful to have God deal with these things as only He can, thus enabling Him to continue to move and flow through His people. Holy boldness has come from the throne room of God and great grace has been received as people have sought God in prayer for the meeting. As we, His people, continue to "pray and obey," God will anoint and will begin to move and we will see Him work in wonderful ways. Through prayer, He works in hearts to lift Himself up and to exalt His Name rather than exalting man. As this happens, He moves and draws people to Himself. Saved and unsaved alike are drawn to Him and the way is made open for His glory to come forth.

UNITY

As we are drawn close to Him, He becomes the center and the focus of everything and we begin to come into the unity of the Spirit. That is where God's blessing is commanded (Psalm 133). The unity of the Spirit focuses on what God is saying and doing and not just what a particular person or group thinks. We, God's people, must first come into unity with His Holy Spirit. As we come into unity with Him, and He is the center, we will find we then will come into unity with each other as God is not against Himself. From this place of unity, we will minister that which the Spirit of God is giving at that particular time and it will minister life to the people. We will not just hammer away at our pet doctrine no matter how wonderful it may be, but we will speak life and minister the life of the Spirit as we come into unity with God and then with each other.

Because we as human beings do not yet walk in the full revelation or knowledge of God, we may not always agree on everything or believe exactly the same way about everything. True unity is not based on this. It is based on Him. Jesus is the focus. As we look to Him, He works in our hearts and the unity of the Spirit begins to come forth. As that happens, God's blessing is commanded and the anointing begins to flow and bring forth the blessing of life.

> *Behold, how good and how pleasant it is for brethren to dwell together in unity!*
> *It is like the precious ointment upon the head, that ran down upon the beard, even Aaron's beard: that went down to the skirts of his garments;*
> *As the dew of Hermon, and as the dew that descended upon the mountains of Zion: ....for there the LORD commanded the blessing, even life forever more.*
>
> —Psalm 133

This scripture regarding the blessing of God being contingent on brothers and sisters dwelling together in unity is crucial! We need the blessing of God in order to prosper in all God has called us to do and be, so that we as individuals can come forth into the fullness of God's plan ourselves. In addition, we need the blessing of God *"even life forevermore"* (Psalm 133:3) in order to effectively minister to those we are called to reach out to. We want to see people truly respond to the life changing gospel of Jesus Christ. We want to see them come into the fullness of God's plan for their lives as they become firmly established in Him.

This promise of God's blessing is also key, especially during times of spiritual opposition as we seek to fulfill the great commission.

> *For we wrestle not against flesh and blood, but against principalities, against powers, against rulers of darkness of this world, against spiritual wickedness in high places.*
> *–Ephesians 6:12*

How wonderful to know that the place of unity is where the blessing of God has been commanded. God's commanded blessing is greater than any curse of darkness. Because Jesus overcame the curse, darkness has to flee as we contend in prayer and stand in faith upon His Word together in unity. Knowing this can be key to praying through for a good meeting, especially when the "war" is on.

The enemy does not want God's plans and purposes to prosper. This is why many times there is opposition prior to God moving. As we go to prayer this opposition can be overcome. As we stand together in unity we will see the enemy defeated. There are many examples of this in Scriptures.

In Judges chapters 6 through 8, we read of the story of Gideon. The children of Israel had been in bondage to the Midianites for seven years. As the children of Israel cried out to the Lord for deliverance, God began to show them why they were in bondage. Then God answered their prayer by raising up a deliverer whose name was Gideon.

Although Gideon felt that he was the "least of the least" and that he was unqualified for the job, he heard what God was saying and obeyed Him. In fact, God spoke to Gideon regarding his feelings about himself and said: *"...Go in this thy might.... Have I not sent thee.... Surely I will be with thee"* (see Judges 6: 14-16). Gideon soon found out that heaven backs those who will hear and obey God.

As Gideon began to believe God and obey God's instructions, God in turn began to show His power. By the end of this story we see that God used Gideon and his army of 300 men, who were in unity with God and His plan as given to Gideon, to defeat about 135,000 heavily armed Midianites (Judges 8:10). Truly God's blessing is commanded in the place of unity!

We see this principle in the New Testament as well. In the book of Acts, chapter 16, we read the story of Paul and Silas. After bringing the Gospel to Philippi, they were arrested and thrown into the innermost part of the jail. The whole city where they were ministering was in an uproar and accused them unjustly of many things.

Paul and Silas were beaten and put in stocks at midnight. What did the other prisoners hear? Did they hear two men who were angry, each one blaming the gods, everyone else or even each other for what had happened? No! They heard Paul and Silas praying and praising the great and mighty God, creator of heaven and earth. God then turned this seemingly hopeless situation around. He sent an earthquake, the prison doors were opened, and yet the prisoners all stayed to hear the Gospel of Jesus Christ and were born again.

It would have been so easy for Paul and Silas to be angry and to get in a fight. They could have blamed each other or blamed the government officials. However, they chose instead to stay in unity with the plan of God and with each other, worshipping and praying to the Lord. From this place of unity God brought forth the blessing of new life — "*even life evermore*" (Psalm 133:3) — as the jailer and his household were saved, (see Acts 16:31-33).

We can learn much from examples such as Gideon, Paul and Silas and others in the Scriptures as we also prepare to see God move in our lives, homes, communities and in our nations. No curse of darkness and no witchcraft can have its way when God's people walk together in unity! We must go forth in unity, first of all with the plan of God and then with those God has called us to walk with. In so doing, we will participate in the miraculous works of God and see His blessings come forth as we meet together in prayer and unity in Jesus Name.

FOUR

ENTERING INTO THE PRESENCE OF GOD

As people begin to gather for the meetings, we will often have pre-service singing by some of the worship team as the people are arriving. Once the people are gathered together and welcomed, we have someone open the meeting in prayer. This helps to bring unity of purpose and releases the presence of God to work in our midst as the people come into agreement and focus on the Lord.

As believers, we truly enter into the presence of God through the blood of Jesus, which washes away our sin and guilt.

> *Having therefore, brethren, boldness to enter into the holiest by the blood of Jesus,*
> *By a new and living way, which he hath consecrated for us, through the veil, that is to say, his flesh;*
> *And having an high priest over the house of God;*
> *Let us draw near with a true heart in full assurance of faith, having our hearts sprinkled*

> *from an evil conscience, and our bodies washed with pure water.*
> —*Hebrews 10:19-22*

When we enter in, we enter into His presence with thanksgiving and praise as we honour and bless His Name. This is the protocol God has given us in His Word for entering into the presence of the King of Kings and Lord of Lords.

> *Enter into His gates with thanksgiving, and into His courts with praise: be thankful unto Him and bless His Name.*
> —*Psalm 100:4*

We come into His presence and create a place for God to dwell in and through our praises.

> *But Thou art holy, O Thou who inhabitest* [lives or dwells] *in the praises of Israel* [i.e., His people].
> —*Psalm 22:3* [emphasis added by author]

I remembered the elders of our assembly in Calgary talking about revival. They had been involved in the 1948 North Battleford outpouring of the Holy Spirit when God moved in life changing revival power. They would talk by the hour of all the wonderful things God did in the meetings and spoke many times regarding the importance of building the Lord a dwelling place through praise and worship. They taught us well! We learned that God would have His people worship Him in Spirit and in truth. We also learned the importance of participating, with all our hearts, in the many forms of worship which are outlined in the Bible and are overviewed later in this chapter.

When we gathered together, we would praise and worship the Lord with all of our hearts and as we did the presence of God would begin to move in an evident way upon the people. As God's tangible presence came, the gifts and anointing of the Holy Ghost would move in and through His people freely. Sometimes God would move with conviction, resulting in people asking for forgiveness and making things right with God and one another. At other times God would move in healing power setting people free from sickness and disease that had bound them for many years. Church was never boring as we would see God move when we would worship Him with all of our hearts.

WE ARE CALLED TO BE A PEOPLE WHO PRAISE AND WORSHIP GOD IN HOLINESS.

Give unto the LORD the glory due unto his name: bring a offering, and Come before him: worship the LORD in the beauty of holiness.
—I Chronicles 16:29

Kings of the earth and all people; princes, and all judges of the earth:
Both young men and maidens; old men, and children:
Let them praise the name of the LORD: for his name alone is excellent; his glory is above the earth and heaven.
—Psalm 148:11-13

> *Let every thing that hath breath praise the LORD. Praise ye the LORD.*
> —Psalm 150:6

Psalm 102: 1-22 gives a wonderful example of how, through praise and worship, God can change how we are feeling about everything.

Commentators are not certain who wrote Psalm 102, however, we do know the writer of this Psalm sounds extremely discouraged in the first 11 verses. Despite all this, in verses 12-22, there is a definite change of tone as the Lord and His greatness is praised. The writer begins to prophesy: God will endure forever, He will be remembered by all generations and He will rise up and have mercy upon his people. The writer also begins to declare that the appointed time of God's favour has come. The author also prophesies: God will appear in his glory, he will hear the prayers of the destitute and that there will be a generation created to praise the Lord. At the time of this occurring the groaning of the prisoner will be heard, there will be a loosing of those appointed to die as God's name is declared. We, the people, will see this come to pass as we come into unity to serve the Lord.

With Rejoicing and Singing

> *I will be glad and rejoice in thee: I will sing praise to thy Name, O thou Most High.*
> —Psalm 9:2

With Joy

> *Make a joyful noise unto the Lord, all ye lands.*
> —Psalm 100:1

With Singing

Come before His presence with singing.
—Psalm 100:2b

Many are the ways in which we praise and worship our Great and Mighty God. Even battles were won as the children of Israel sang, praised and worshipped God. In response God's presence began to move amongst them.

It is interesting to note that when Israel was in obedience to God, they were always victorious in battle. Seventy eight of these battles are recorded in scripture. Each victory was unique as God directed the battle strategy. So it is in praise and worship. As we go before he Lord he will give us the songs and direction of the worship as well as battle strategies. His strategies will always work when we are in obedience to Him

With Singing New Songs:
(a song that God gives)

Praise the Lord, sing unto the Lord a new song.
—Psalm 149:1, Psalm 98:1

In the Dance

This is a dance that is done to worship God. It is not usually a learned or a practiced dance. It is not a worldly dance. People often begin to dance spontaneously as the presence of God comes. It is not for people, but for God.

Let them praise His name in the dance.
—Psalm 149:3a…

Praise Him with the timbrel and dance.
—Psalm 150:4a…

In 1 Chronicles 15 there is a beautiful story about the return of the Ark of the Covenant to Israel. This is so significant for with the Ark of the Covenant came the presence of God.

Led by the priests, the children of Israel celebrated with great joy, singing, as well as with musical instruments and dancing as the presence of God returned. King David danced before the Lord with all of his might and the presence of the Lord was restored to the people. Not everyone was happy because of the noise and the exuberance of the praise, however, God was pleased and God blessed the people and the Kingdom greatly. Many battles were supernaturally won in the days to come, and God continued to bless the children of Israel as they continued to worship and walk in obedience to God, allowing His presence to lead them.

We can learn much from this example in the Scriptures. As we the church of the Living God, learn to worship Him with all of our might, we also will see His presence come in unprecedented measure. Our God inhabits the praises of His people [Psalm 22:3].

With our Musical Instruments

Praise him for his mighty acts: praise him according to his excellent greatness.
Praise him with the sound of the trumpet: praise him with the psaltery and harp.
Praise him with the timbrel and dance: praise him with stringed instruments and organs.
—Psalm 150:3-5

With Shouting and Weeping

Ezra 3:9-13 gives the account of a "praise and worship service" in which musical instruments, singing, giving of thanks, shouting and weeping, as well as joy, were all a part of the service.

> *...And all the people shouted with a great shout, when they praised the Lord, because the foundation of the house of the Lord was laid ....when the foundation of this house was laid before their eyes, wept with a loud voice; and many shouted aloud for joy.*
>
> *—Ezra 3:11b and 12b*

****

When we praise God the powers of darkness are driven back and defeated. An excellent example of this is found in 2 Chronicles 20:14-25. Here we read the account of King Jehoshaphat and the people of Judah who were surrounded by the enemy armies. He knew that without God's intervention they were already defeated. As Jehoshaphat and all of Judah began to worship the Lord and pray for deliverance, the Spirit of God began to move. God gave him and the people the battle strategy for victory. Their awesome miracle of deliverance is recorded in 2 Chronicles,

> *And when they began to sing and to praise, the Lord set ambushments against the children of Ammon, Moab, and mount Seir, which were come against Judah; and they were smitten.*
>
> *—2 Chronicles 20:22*

Praise God, as the singers began to worship and praise the Lord, the enemy was utterly defeated even though they far outnumbered the army of Judah.

As heartfelt praise comes forth in meetings today, the enemy and his plans are destroyed as God's presence is loosed. God's spirit then begins to move. The people become free to receive from the Lord. Praise is a powerful weapon and it opens the doors for God to come in power amongst His people.

Oftentimes when a meeting is difficult, either because of distractions or a feeling of heaviness, we find that the spirit of oppression is in operation. This spirit comes to try and shut down what God would do in the service. It has to go when we begin to praise Him with all our hearts. Though it is the enemy who tries to bind a service up, united praise can break the power of darkness and bring release to God's people.

Another difficulty small groups may encounter is that there are times when there is no one available to play a musical instrument during worship. It is important not to be discouraged. When this happens, we can still praise and worship God with all our might with singing, as well as in other ways. We can clap or use a tambourine while singing. In situations like this we have seen God come forth in great blessing as people have entered in, praising and singing with all their hearts. As they sang out with all their might, God helped people overcome their self consciousness, and became God conscious instead. Often when this occurred, He moved powerfully! It is not our great talent or our magnificent sound system or the quality of the instruments that brings the presence of God, although these things are wonderful when used for His glory. Above all, God seeks the worship of His people who will worship Him in Spirit and in truth.

> *But the hour cometh, and now is when the true worshipers shall worship the Father in spirit and in truth: for the Father seeketh such to worship Him.*
> *God is a Spirit: and they that worship Him must worship Him in spirit and in truth.*
> *—John 4:23-24*

He calls us to worship Him from the heart with all of our being. Even if we do not have instruments, we will still worship and exalt Him. With our instruments or without them, we will worship Him in spirit and in truth and we will make His praise glorious for He alone is worthy!

FIVE

THE MOVING OF GOD'S SPIRIT

As the Spirit of God begins to move, He will move on people in many different ways. For our part, we begin responding to God by praising and worshipping Him with all of our hearts. As our hearts open to Him, increasingly our response will be orchestrated by His Spirit. At times there may be singing or weeping or shouting, or a "holy hush" may come and people will be quiet before Him as His Spirit settles upon them. As people respond to God, the anointing begins to flow upon His people and God often begins to move in supernatural ways. We have seen people begin to march or shout and as this happens people have been delivered from various bondages. At other times a stillness or weeping has come and people have been healed. In one service I remember the Spirit of God falling in great conviction on some of the teenage boys; spontaneously, one by one, they came forward weeping to receive prayer and salvation. This happened without an altar call as people were worshipping God with songs from their hearts to Him.

As we wait on God, He may speak through a vision or through the gifts of the Spirit (see 1 Corinthians 12). There are times when a word of knowledge, a word of wisdom, a message in tongues and interpretation of tongues, prophetic words or songs of the Holy Spirit may flow through His people. Someone may also play an instrument in the Spirit which is a supernatural anointing to play a song that has not been learned. The body of Christ is strengthened, edified and increased when God moves in these ways. How much we miss if we do not wait upon Him for His will to come forth.

God can move in so many ways. The key is to be open to Him and to His order for the service and for each person to go in the direction in which He moves. It is His will for the meeting that is desired. It is exciting to be in these services for God can use anyone at any time no matter how young or old, and as we wait on Him, His direction and order begins to come forth. As we learn to yield to Him, it is a wonderful thing to see the hand of God and His plan come forth instead of the programs of man.

As the presence of God comes and He begins to move and to anoint different people, it is good to ask God for His clear direction and timing. If everyone is praising the Lord and worshipping with all their hearts and the anointing comes on an individual to sing a prophetic song or to prophesy, many would not hear it if it was delivered while everyone was still praising and worshipping God. However, if the person learns to hold the anointing and to keep focused on Jesus, God will make a way for them to bring forth the word or song when people can hear it. A lull will often come as the corporate praising slows and then the special song or word can be heard. Often after a song or songs come by the Spirit, the Song of the Lord will continue corporately, and then another lull will come. Others may have songs or prophecies which they then would bring forth during these lulls.

It is also good to wait on the Lord before changing the order of the service until you are certain God is not anointing someone to bring forth something else which is relevant at that time. As people learn to stay in unity and focus on God's plan: His plan and His order will come forth. His blessing will then flow in the meeting. It is not enough that He just comes; we want the completion of what He wants to do throughout the entire meeting and in every heart and life.

Sometimes, as we have been waiting on God, it is evident that the Spirit of God is moving on someone and the anointing is upon them to minister, but they are shy to speak. Perhaps they are just beginning and are uncertain of what to do. One of the joys of open meetings is time can be taken to go and to stand beside them as God leads, thus encouraging them to bring forth what God is giving them. We have found it is good not to rush but to take time. We have seen many begin to come forth under a powerful anointing in tongues and interpretation, prophecy, as well as speaking forth a vision or word that God has given. As we have waited upon the Lord and encouraged them to take those first steps of faith we have seen God move in some wonderful ways. Just as it takes a baby time to take his first steps, so it takes time for people to learn to minister under the anointing of God. Along with seeking God, it takes time and experience — and often support, instruction and encouragement — to learn to walk it out. What better place is there than in the local assembly for the people to take these steps? Is it not the local assembly where His people should be trained up for the work of the ministry?

> *And He gave some, apostles; and some, prophets; and some, evangelists; and some, pastors and teachers; For the perfecting of the saints, for the work of the ministry, for the edifying of the body of Christ:*
> *Till we all come in the unity of the faith, and of the knowledge of the Son of God, unto a perfect man, unto the measure of the stature of the fullness of Christ:*
> *That we henceforth be no more children, tossed to and fro, and carried about by every wind of doctrine, by the sleight of men, and cunning craftiness, whereby they lie in wait to deceive;*
> *But speaking the truth in love, may grow up into Him all things, which is the head, even Christ:*
> *From whom the whole body fitly joined together and compacted by that which every joint supplieth, according to the effectual working in the measure of every part, maketh increase of the body unto the edifying of itself in love.*
> *—Ephesians 4:11-16*

Being perfected for the work of the ministry is crucial. That which every joint and every part supplies is so important as each person learns to effectively minister as part of the body. Through this the body of Christ is matured, edified, strengthened and increased. New ministries are birthed as people minister the things of God.

Often the church is pictured as a living body. Just as it is important for every part of our body to function in order to be healthy, so it is in the body of Christ. As each person waits on God and gives what God shows him or her to share; a vibrant, healthy church, flowing with the life of God begins to emerge.

As God has moved through His people we have witnessed some awesome ministries come forth and have also experienced some very powerful meetings. One such meeting that comes to mind was held in a small isolated village along the Mackenzie River in Northern Canada. We had travelled many hours by boat to bring the gospel tent into the village. As the various members of the team ministered the word and testimony, God began to move in hearts and people began to respond. Many people gave their hearts to Jesus.

A man who was extremely drunk came for prayer. As the team prayed he became totally sober, repented and asked the Lord to save him. He was delivered and set free! He then went back home and brought his children back to the meeting. His three children, his mother and his estranged wife got saved that night.

As members of the team ministered to this family, the children were healed from the hurt, anger and rejection that they had experienced from their father. His mother was able to forgive her son for years of rebellion and hurt. He and his wife, who also had received the baptism of the Holy Spirit that evening, were reconciled after they both had received ministry from different team members.

While all this was going on, others were getting touched as well. Salvation, healing and deliverance flowed freely. The lay reader from a church which did not believe in personal salvation gave his heart to the Lord. Another elder got up publicly to say, "I don't know who these people are, or where they came from, but this Jesus they talk about — He really works"… Truly He does and it is wonderful to see Him do so.

From the team that travelled with us, God has raised up three pastors, an evangelist, a preacher/intercessor who moves in prophetic ministry, and a prophetic worship leader/preach-teacher. It is awesome to see what God does through body ministry. God not only ministers to the needs of the people but also brings people forth in their ministry.

Since my early days in Calgary at the hall to the present day, I have been so privileged to witness many come forth in ministry as they have ministered within the local assembly and have taken their place in the body of Christ.

SIX

OPEN SHARING AND BODY MINISTRY

As God's people continue to be open to the leading of the Holy Spirit, God will show how He wants to proceed in the meeting. Following a time of worship, usually there will be a time of open sharing followed by preaching/teaching and prayer for special needs. It may not necessarily all be in that order, but God will show step by step what He wants as His people look to Him.

The term open meetings, usually implies some type of open sharing. Although there may occasionally be exceptions to this (i.e. a special series of teaching meetings during week nights when time may be limited and the emphasis is on the teaching). However, apart from these occasional agreed upon exceptions, open meetings have a time of open sharing for believers. Open sharing includes special songs, testimonies and exhortations from God's Word.

It is beneficial for people to share because God's life flows through His Body and every part is so valuable (see Ephesians 4:16). Encourage people to share, wait on them to do so, and then listen as the different ones endeavour to bring forth what God has given them. As we receive from one another that which the Lord has given, we are all encouraged and edified. We will often be amazed at how God brings it all together. As we receive from each other the gifts He has given, we also receive from Him.

Ephesians 4:15-16 shows us that every joint is to fill it's purpose and in so doing, the body is increased (see Appendix A). This increase of souls, saved for His glory comes from God is what is needed if we are going to see the church be fruitful and multiply in this hour.

We also learn from Paul in the book of 1 Corinthians that we are to strengthen or edify each other in the body of Christ. Each person has a role to play in this.

> *...When ye come together everyone of you hath a psalm, hath a doctrine, hath a tongue, hath a revelation, hath an interpretation. Let all things be done unto edifying.*
> *–1 Corinthians 14:26*

Praise God, as we seek Him, He will give each one of us something to contribute. May we learn to allow God to bring these things forth in us and through us. The flesh and the enemy would like to see many other things happen rather than this, but as we allow God to cleanse us, to teach us, to fill us and to use us, we will be thrilled to see what He does as His plans come forth.

It is absolutely vital that the people be taught that the meeting time is not the place for rambling or visiting. If we are visiting, we can't hear what God is speaking to us through His people. Not only that but we can also hinder others from hearing and receiving what God has for them. It is best for everyone to know that *visiting is for after the meeting*. The meeting is the time for each one to share in turn that which God has given them to edify (make strong and build) the body. If God has given them something to say to us, surely we do not want to miss it.

Each part of the body is incredibly valuable. A body in which only the head works is quadriplegic. God is raising up a healthy vibrant bride. Every part must learn to function under God and we, the Church, need the strength that comes from this.

> *Let the word of Christ dwell in you [not just the preacher] richly in all wisdom; teaching and admonishing one another in psalms and hymns and spiritual songs, singing with grace in your hearts to the Lord.*
> *–Colossians 3:16 [insertion by author]*

Short, powerful testimonies and exhortations from the Word of God during open sharing can be a real blessing. These testimonies of what Jesus has done truly help to overcome and to defeat the enemy and his lies, both in our own lives and in the lives of others. We need to both listen to and to share these testimonies and exhortations of the power of Jesus. We learn in the Word that, "…*They overcame him* [the accuser of the brethren—Satan] *by the blood of the Lamb and by the word of their testimony…*" (Revelation 12:11, (brackets and emphasis by author).

Unless the leader has specifically asked for a "life story" (a long) testimony, it is best to ask God *what part* of your testimony He would have you to share. The Holy Spirit knows the heart and the needs of each person in the meeting. He can give you exactly what is needed to see someone set free, edified or encouraged. Keep it short and "salty" so that people will want more of what you have from the Lord. It is not a time for the "moanies." It is a time to share how Jesus has helped you or is helping you and can help others, too! This way we continue to glorify God and to build up the body of Christ. Your areas of special need can be ministered to during the prayer and ministry time. If a need is immediate, share this with the leader so it can be dealt with. What you have from God is important and should be shared as He leads. The meeting time is the time for God to use you and each one for His glory, to say or to do what God would have each person say or do in the meeting.

What others have to share from God is also very important and should also be listened to. Sometimes people forget that in open meetings God will often give pieces of the "puzzle" to different people. Therefore, if we are going to see the whole picture, it is vital to receive that which He has given to others and not just to ourselves. We are instructed in His Word to:

> *Let nothing be done through strife or vainglory;*
> *but in lowliness of mind let each esteem other*
> *better than themselves,*
> *Look not every man on his own things, but*
> *every man also on the things of others.*
> *—Philippians 2:3, 4*

Not only do we want to be heard when we share our testimonies but we also need to hear others who are sharing. If we do not, several things can happen. First, our disrespect may grieve the Holy Spirit who is moving through them. Neither do we want to miss out on what God would minister through others to us. In addition, we want to honour the Lord in the vessels He chooses to use. When we are not open to receive from them, without actually intending to, we may communicate to others that what they have is not important or valid.

I remember a time when God was moving on one of the reserves in an incredible way. A team had approached us and asked if we would take them to the reserve as they wanted to minister to the people there. We drove several hours to get to the service and when we arrived, the meeting was well underway. People were worshipping God with all their hearts. When the service opened up for the body ministry the team got up and shared. When they sat down they said, "Let's go home now it's getting late." I said, "No." I knew their departure would be seen as disrespectful. I also knew that God was moving. The team would perhaps receive a touch from the Lord - if they settled down and realized that what God gave others was also important and that they could receive as well as give.

At first the team leader was not too happy, but it didn't last. What happened next was absolutely awesome. As the people from the reserve began to move out in faith and minister what God had given them, God began to come in power. The Spirit of God was moving so strongly that about 25 people went forward to give their hearts to Jesus. The team that had come with us began to weep as they saw God moving in such a way. What was so precious was that the leader of the meeting on the reserve came and asked them if they would like to pray with the young people at the altar which they did. God began to flow through the visiting team as well. I am sure from what they later shared, that lives were forever impacted as they experienced God moving through them as they prayed and saw people weeping and repenting as they got right with God and with each other. The meeting continued till four o'clock in the morning. Even the children began to dance and worship God when the joy of the Lord began to break out amongst the people. How wonderful it is to receive from the Lord the blessings He longs to pour out through His many-membered body!

SEVEN

TEACHING AND PREACHING GOD'S WORD

We are called to preach and teach God's holy and infallible Word.

Usually there is a time, over and above the open sharing, designated for teaching or preaching the Word of God in the meeting. The one who has the responsibility to teach or preach for any particular meeting is under the authority of the leader and the leader is responsible under God to pray for God's choice for the meeting. Although others may have shared a scripture, a revelation from the Word or an exhortation, there is still room for the "main course." Each part of a Spirit-led meeting is important and will complement and not take away from the other. Along with the moving of God's Spirit, we need the life-giving, anointed Word of God! It is His Word that God confirms as is shown in the book of Mark.

> *And they went forth, and preached every where, the Lord working with them, and confirming the Word with signs following, Amen*
>
> *—Mark 16:20*

We see this so clearly when we study the writings of Paul to his spiritual son Timothy, when he states:

> *All scripture is given by inspiration of God, and is profitable for doctrine, for reproof, for correction, for instruction in righteousness: That the man of God may be perfect, thoroughly furnished unto all good works.*
>
> *—2 Timothy 3:16-17*

The words of Jesus instruct and encourage those who are called to teach and preach. He said to those following Him,

> *...Go ye therefore and teach all nations... teaching them to observe all things whatsoever I have commanded you...*
>
> *—Matthew 28:18-20*

Again, in Mark 16:15 we read, "*Go ye into all the world and preach the gospel...*" We are asked to go and teach and preach the Word of God, and as we do, Jesus also promises to confirm His Word with signs following (see Mark 16:16-19). In Mark 16:20 we read how "*...the Lord....confirmed the Word with signs following*" as the disciples preached and taught the Word of God.

God confirms His Word with signs following and through this He prepares hearts to receive from Him. It is so important for God's Word to come forth in meetings and to be valued and received as His Word.

BENEFITS OF GOD'S WORD

A beautiful overview which shows the benefits and the power as well as why we need God's Word can be read in Psalm 119. In this incredible Psalm of David, nearly every verse describes the benefits of God's Word. Two of my favourite verses are found in this Psalm. In this Psalm we find an answer for our struggle with sin and darkness. There are other scriptures as well that teach us why we so desperately need to hear and receive God's Word.

God's Word Helps Us Overcome Sin

> *Thy Word have I hid in mine heart, that I might not sin against thee.*
>
> *—Psalm 119:11*

God's Word Overcomes Our Darkness

> *Thy word is a lamp unto my feet, and a light unto my path*
>
> *—Psalm 119:105*

God's Word Is Powerful

> *For the word of God is quick, and powerful, and sharper than any two-edged sword, piercing even to the dividing asunder of soul and spirit, and of the joints and marrow, and is a discerner of the thoughts and intents of the heart.*
>
> *—Hebrews 4:12*

Lives are forever changed when God's word and the Spirit of God is allowed to do its work. A wonderful example of this happening can be seen in the life of Jonathan Edwards whom God used mightily during the great awakening to see thousands of souls come to God. As usual Jonathan Edwards read this sermon in a monotone voice, however, God began to move in a very unusual way. This move began at a place called Enfield on July 8th, 1741.

Jonathan Edwards: *"Sinners in the Hands of an Angry God."*

Text: Their foot shall slide in due time. –Deut. 32:35.

> *Enfield, July 8th, 1741*
>
> *"On this day in history, Jonathan Edwards started a sermon that he did not finish. Such was the impact of his preaching that the people listening shrieked and cried out, and the crying and weeping became so loud that Edwards was forced to discontinue the sermon. Instead, the pastors went down among the people and prayed with them in groups. Many came to a saving knowledge of Christ that day."* [2]

God's Word Arouses Faith

> *Faith comes by hearing and hearing by the word of God.*
>
> *—Romans 10:17*

---

2   Crossway.Org This Day in History: Jonathan Edwards Preaches "Sinners in the Hands of an Angry God"

God's Word Reconciles—(brings people together to God and to each other)

> [God]...*hath committed unto us the word of reconciliation.*
> —2 Corinthians 5:19 [insertion by the author]

God's Word Washes Us

> ...*Christ...gave Himself for it* [the church]
> *That He might sanctify and cleanse it with the washing of water by the Word,*
> *That He might present it to Himself a glorious church, not having spot or wrinkle, or any such thing; but that it should be holy and without blemish.*
> Ephesians 5:25-27 [insertion by the author]

God's Word Gives Life

> ... *Ye shine as lights in the world; holding forth the word of life....*
> —Philippians 2: 15-16

> ... *The words that I speak unto you, they are Spirit and are life.*
> —John 6:63

God's Word Teaches Us

> *All scripture is given by inspiration of God, and is profitable for doctrine, for reproof, for correction, for instruction in righteousness, that*

> *the man of God may be perfect, thoroughly furnished unto all good works.*
> 			—2 Timothy 3:16-17

God's Word teaches us many things. It is through the Word of God that we come to know Him and receive eternal life. We also learn about the character of God and come to know what He likes and does not like, as well as what pleases Him and what does not. Through His Word we learn; that when we come to the saving knowledge of Jesus Christ. It is through continuing in it, that we will walk in freedom. Truly His Word is powerful and changes lives for time and eternity.

God's Word Heals Us and Delivers Us

> *He sent His word, and healed them, and delivered them from their destructions.*
> 			—Psalms 107:20

God's Word Causes Us to Grow

> *As newborn babes, desire the sincere milk of the Word that ye may grow thereby.*
> 			—1 Peter 2:2

As babies truly desire milk, so we ought to desire the Word. Even as a mother's milk makes a baby strong, develops the immune system and releases antibodies against infection, so the Word of God strengthens us, heals us and keeps us from the infectious wiles of Satan, if we will allow it to do its work.

God's Word Roots and Establishes Us

As ye have therefore received Christ Jesus the Lord, so walk ye in Him: rooted and built up in Him, and established in the faith as ye have been taught...
  —Colossians 2:6-7

God's Word Teaches Us the Secrets of Good Success

The key is in observing, meditating, speaking and doing all that the Word of God instructs us to do.

...Then thou shalt make thy way prosperous and then thou shalt have good success.
  —Joshua 1:8b

Who doesn't want to be a success. We can learn a lot from Joshua. Joshua knew what it was to succeed. He knew what God said believed it and obeyed it. The Bible records many of his victories. He was one of the twelve leaders chosen to spy out the promised land prior to taking the children of Israel in to conquer it. God had told them the land was already given to them and gave them instructions on what to do. Joshua and Caleb believed God's word and were able to withstand the negative peer pressure of the other ten spy's and approximately two and a half million people who did not believe God's Word. The other ten spies and all the adults who did not believe it died in the wilderness, whereas Joshua and Caleb had faith in what God said. They successfully led all the young people into the land as God had promised.

God's Word is Awesome

It is worth taking time to prayerfully read Psalm 119, which is the longest Psalm in the Bible. It tells us so much about the power of God's Word. This is what we all need in our lives and in our meetings.

We have seen some wonderful things happen as God's Word, bathed in prayer, has gone forth through His many-membered body. At times we have seen salvation come, healings occur, people set free from chains of bondage and their lives totally changed as God has come and touched them through the power of His Word. We also have experienced the joy of seeing lives become rooted and grounded in Christ and over time we have seen leaders raised up and established as God's Word has been given under the anointing by young and old alike.

Many of the smaller meetings may not have access to "big name" preachers, but as God's people learn to lift up The Biggest Name of All, signs and wonders truly follow! God will never leave "high and dry" a people who scripturally seek after Him with all their hearts.

EIGHT

SPECIAL PRAYER FOR SALVATION, HEALING AND OTHER NEEDS

We read in the book of Romans that: "*...faith cometh by hearing and hearing by the Word of God*" (Romans 10:17).

Concerning prayer for special needs, we read in the book of Mark that, *"these signs shall follow them that believe, in My name"* (Jesus said) *"they shall cast out devils."* He also said, *"they shall lay hands on the sick and they shall recover"* (see Mark 16:17-18). In Mark 16:20 we learn that that is exactly what happened. No wonder the Scriptures say:

> *Is any among you afflicted? let him pray...*
> *Is any sick among you? Let him call for the elders of the church; and let them pray over him...*
> *And the prayer of faith shall save the sick, and the Lord shall raise him up, and if he have committed sins, they shall be forgiven him.*
> *Confess your faults one to another, and pray one for another, that ye may healed. The effectual*

> *fervent prayer of a righteous man availeth much.*
> *Elias...prayed earnestly that it might not rain: and it rained not on the earth by the space of three years and six months.*
> *And he prayed again, and the heaven gave rain, and the earth brought forth her fruit.*
> –James 5:13-18

We serve a God who hears and answers prayer! We read in Psalm 65:2 "*O thou that hearest prayer, unto thee shall all flesh come.*" Jeremiah states,

> *Call upon Me and I will answer thee and show thee great and mighty things which thou knowest not.*
> –Jeremiah 33:3

God does not say He *might* answer us, He says He *will* answer us. We, as God's children, need to continually step out in faith and believe God together for the fulfillment of His Word both personally and in meetings when we pray for the needs of one another.

Therefore, it is important to set time aside to pray for special needs such as salvation, healing, deliverance and the baptism of the Holy Spirit. Those that believe should lay hands on the people who desire prayer and pray. Everyone should come into agreement, as prayer is being made, for God commands His blessing when we dwell together in unity (see Psalm 133).

It is often beneficial during this time to ask people with a burden for the sick to help pray. This is a wonderful way for people to learn to pray for the sick as they link up with those who are more experienced in this type of prayer. It is also important that those praying together learn the power of agreement in prayer. Often gifts of healing will begin to manifest as people are encouraged to enter in. Both the vessel and the person receiving prayer are blessed. God will move through the body of believers as people are allowed to exercise their faith. When praying in a group like this, it is good to wait on God and on each other to hear what God is saying to the various ones ministering. As time is given for this, people will learn to minister and flow together as the Lord moves through His many-membered body.

As young people in our assembly, we were taught to agree with those who were praying for the sick. Often we were called up to the front to help lay hands on the sick and to agree in prayer with those who were actually praying over them. We would pray silently and believe God to really touch the people. It was good training.

One day, as we were worshiping and waiting in the presence of God, our pastor began to speak in another language. We had heard him do this before, however, this time it went on for about 20 minutes. We were amazed. His wife then got up and interpreted what had been said. She also spoke for about 20 minutes. When she sat down the atmosphere was electric! We were so immersed in the presence of God that we didn't realize that after the service had started, approximately 30 First Nations people from a nearby reserve had come into the service.

It turned out that our pastor had been speaking in the Blackfoot language, and his wife had then interpreted what he had been saying. Everyone knew that in the natural, our pastors could not speak a word of Blackfoot nor did they understand it, however, later the people shared that the Blackfoot and the interpretation had been perfect.

All of a sudden there were people everywhere as people came running to the altar in response to the invitation that God had given. People were both crying and laughing, getting right with God, praying, interceding and some were rejoicing. So many wanted prayer. Because of the number of people wanting prayer, the pastor released the young people who had been trained to quietly agree in prayer while they were praying for the sick to come up to the front and minister freely to the people.

What an incredible day that was. We saw God move! I remember a lady coming for prayer who had a great big hole in one of her teeth. God filled it that day and we watched while it was happening — it was awesome. We saw young children, some as young as three years old, get baptized with the Holy Spirit. Another lady had a large tumor which absolutely disappeared as God's presence touched her.

This move of God went on for several hours and the people were rejoicing that God loved them enough to speak to them in their own language and minister to them in such a very special way. We were thrilled too. It was wonderful to see God moving through so many of His people in such wonderful ways that day.

In a larger open meeting, not everyone will be involved with the laying on of hands at the altar. It is still important, however, that the people be taught to come into agreement with those who are praying and save visiting until the end of the meeting. In this way everyone is still involved with the meeting and the unity of the Spirit will prevail. It is in this atmosphere that the blessing and presence of God will move. His will is accomplished as we honour Him and His word in faith believing.

When the time of ministry and the service itself is completed, close in prayer. There are several things that can be included in this prayer. In Mark 4:4&14-15, Jesus teaches us that our adversary, Satan, will try and steal the Word that has been given. Therefore it is important to pray that the Holy Spirit seal God's Word in hearts so it will not be stolen but will be fruitful instead. As well, the closing prayer provides a wonderful opportunity to pray blessing over the congregation and also the community where the meeting is being held.

NINE

WHY WE MEET TOGETHER

The question has been asked, "*Do we really need to meet together as believers?*" In order to answer this question, we need to look in Scriptures and see what they say to us. There are several analogies, or word pictures, by which the Lord describes His people.

When Jesus was teaching in the book of Matthew, He referred to His people as both salt and light:

> *Ye are the salt of the earth...*
> *ye are the light of the world. A city that is set on a hill cannot be hid."*
>
> —*Matthew 5:13a-14*

A single grain of salt alone will do little. However, when combined with other grains of salt it will enhance the taste of food, will preserve food, will make people thirsty and has cleansing and healing properties. It needs the other grains of salt to truly be effective.

I was 13 years old when I met some Christian young people. They were so caring and vibrant. Their joy was infectious. I found myself strangely drawn to them even though I was a part of a very different crowd. As I got to know them more. I wanted to be like them and to be a part of them. Put in scriptural terms; I began to hunger and thirst for what they had. Today, though many years have passed, I still remember the influence they had upon me. They were used by God as salt in my life, forever impacting me and making me hungry and thirsty for something better than this world offers.

God will use His people in these ways, but in order to do the job well, we need each other. In the same way, a city is not just one house with a light, but many houses with many lights. In the darkness of night, the light of the city shines brightly and cannot be easily hid. So it is with us, as we come together, the light of Christ brightly shines out into the darkness through His people to those who are lost in the darkness can truly see it.

In 1st Peter we read:

> *Ye also, as lively stones, are built up a spiritual house, an holy priesthood, to offer up spiritual sacrifices, acceptable to God by Jesus Christ.*
> *–I Peter 2:5*

In this scripture, Peter describes God's people in two ways. First of all, he calls us lively stones which are brought together for a specific purpose. These stones, which are a picture of us, are called to build up a spiritual house. This house is called the temple and it will hold the manifest presence of Almighty God. A house or temple is built with many stones, not just one stone. The stones have to come together and be formed to fit together in order to make a house and so it is with God's people. There has to be a coming together of the "lively stones" in order to become a temple of the living God which will show forth God's glory in this hour.

In 1 Peter 2:5, Peter also pictures God's people as a holy priesthood. A priesthood is not just one priest but many priests. Each one has a specific job to do as individuals, however, they work together for a common cause. Again, so it is with God's people; we are part of a larger body and as such, although we all have different jobs to do, we work together in His Kingdom in order to accomplish the work of the Lord.

In the Scriptures, believers are also pictured as a many-membered body. Just as a body needs all its different parts to fully function, so we need each other (see 1 Corinthians 12:12-27). Paul, writing to the Romans, exhorted them saying:

> *For as we have many members in one body, and all members have not the same office: So we, being many, are one body in Christ, and every one members one of another.*
> —*Romans 12:4-5*

In the book of Hebrews we are exhorted to:

> *Let us consider one another to provoke unto love and good works:*
> *Not forsaking the assembling of ourselves together, as a manner of some is; but exhorting one another: and so much the more, as you see the day approaching.*
> —*Hebrews 10:24-25*

As we have seen, the plans and purposes of God are accomplished more effectively when we come together. Together we can do far more than one individual can do alone.

The place where God has called us together with other believers becomes a place of refuge for us. Even animals in the wild have an understanding of this. When a wolf comes, he will try and cut his prey off from the main herd and when he does so, he knows lunch is about to be served. So it is with the enemy. If he can cut us off from the rest of the believers so that we are alone with no support and no accountability, we become easy prey for him to take advantage of us. However, God's blessing, *"even life forever more,"* is commanded where His children come together and dwell in unity (see Psalm 133).

We need to function together as a body with other believers and also we need time alone with God (see Matthew 6:6) to pray and seek His face. Both help to bring God's balance into our lives so that His Kingdom purposes are fulfilled.

We minister in northern Canada and have been asked, "What do we do when there is no church in our community and the next community is a 3 to 5 hours drive away?" Or, "I live in a community which is isolated except for travel by plane or boat. How can I meet together with other believers and have church?" These are excellent questions. It was questions such as these that prompted the writing of this book.

In some communities enough believers have come to the Lord to see a church or small group get established. Some other alternatives that have been helpful are the use of Skype, bush radio, and local radio stations in some of the northern communities. We have had some wonderful testimonies regarding the use of these means of communication from those who are in isolated situations. We have actually had long distance telephone or skype meetings with believers from communities in B.C., the Northwest Territories, Alberta, and Saskatchewan all joining in together and it has been awesome. Together we enjoyed worship, testimonies, sharing of God's Word and prayer for special needs. How precious these phone meetings have been. When God makes a way for people to come together what a time of rejoicing there is.

TEN

DETERMINING WHERE AND WHEN TO MEET

Our example is the early church. The early church met in many different places. For instance we know that the early church met in the temple and also in homes. We read in Acts 5.

And daily in the temple and in every house, they ceased not to teach and preach Jesus Christ.
–Acts 5:42

They also met outside or wherever else God led, for example, in jail (see Acts 16:13-34).

We can learn many things from the story of Paul and Silas as recorded in Acts 16. In Chapter 3 of this book we discussed the power of praise and worship from this account. Now we are going to focus on a different aspect of the story as told in Acts 16. When determining where and when we meet as believers, we have some helpful models portrayed in scripture. Acts 16 is one of these. In the book of Acts 16:13-15, we read the story of Paul meeting with some women by the riverside. The women had been meeting there to worship God and to pray. When Paul went to that meeting, he explained the way of salvation to those assembled there and Lydia and all her household were baptized. These were the meetings that birthed the church in Philippi.

Shortly thereafter, Paul and Silas were arrested and put in jail after a demon-possessed girl was set free by the power of God. When they were in jail, they still continued meeting, worshipping and praising God and seeing people come to Jesus. We read in Acts:

> *And at midnight Paul and Silas prayed, and sang praises unto God: and the prisoners heard them...*
> *And they* [Paul and Silas] *said, Believe on the Lord Jesus Christ, and thou shalt be saved, and thy house.*
> *And they spake unto him the word of the Lord, and to all that were in his house.*
> *And he took them the same hour of the night, and washed their stripes; and was baptized, he and all his, straightway.*
> *And when he had brought them into his house, he set meat before them, and rejoiced, believing in God with all his house.*
> —*Acts 16:25, 31-34* [insertion by author]

It did not matter to the early church whether they met in temples, in houses, in jails, or on river banks. It did not, nor does it, take a specific type of building to have or be a thriving, God-ordained church. The emphasis of the church was not the building; the emphasis was on the people being the church. They preached and taught whenever and wherever God gave the opportunity, secure in the knowledge that *they* were the church and the meeting place was just that—a meeting place to meet with God. That, and not the building or the lack thereof, was the important factor. A building did not legitimize them as a "church." *They* were the church—a living vibrant body of believers all of whom had an important God-given part in what God was doing in and through His people.

ELEVEN

TWENTY-FOUR/SEVEN CHRISTIANITY

Because of what God was doing in and through the early church, many believers gave themselves to God 24/7. There was no division or distinction between "secular life" and "church life." Sunday-only Christianity was unknown for most believers because they were putting their lives at risk of martyrdom even to be called a Christian. If they worked in secular employment, it was for God's purposes just as preaching or other activities were. Wherever they worked or served became a God-given opportunity to believe the Lord for His plans and purposes to be accomplished. It was almost as if there was a sign over the inside exit door of every meeting place which said, "*Welcome to the mission field.*"

No wonder communities were transformed by the life-changing power of God. May we see the same again today as members of the body of Christ lay hold of the fact that we have a high and holy calling—24/7.

A commitment to 24/7 Christianity often happens with people who have been involved in open meetings as they have received much from the Lord as they sought

Him in prayer. As God begins to minister to and through them they realize that God does not want to use them just in meetings—as wonderful as that may be. He wants to do so much more.

He also has a call upon each of his children. When we yield to His plan, we find it will encompass our entire lives. When this happens, life takes on a new purpose, excitement and meaning. As we seek God with all of our heart we will find Him and also His plan will begin to unfold.

> *For I know the thoughts that I think toward you, saith the Lord, thoughts of peace, and not of evil, to give you an expected end.*
> *Then shall ye call upon me, and ye shall go and pray unto me, and I will hearken unto you.*
> *And ye shall seek me, and find me, when ye shall search for me with all your heart.*
> *–Jeremiah 29:11-13*

God wants to use each one of us for His Glory and to see lives and communities again transformed by the power of God. His power flowing through each part of His many-membered body—all who are willing to take up their cross 24/7 and to follow Him.

TWELVE

MEETING TOGETHER AS A BODY OF BELIEVERS

It is imperative to remember that we are a part of the Body of Christ and we meet as a body of believers. Every part is important (please review 1 Corinthians 12:4-27). Each part of the body is unique and has a unique part to play. Some parts are more visible than others, but a body needs its "hidden" parts to function as well. Each part should be encouraged and valued. The anointing will not flow as freely in and through the preachers in the pulpit without the private intercession of the prayer warriors.

Ministries cannot go into the harvest fields unless they are sent. God uses people to both pray and to give so that others may be released to go and minister in the harvest fields and the vineyard of the Lord. Whether we are called to pray, to preach, to work, to give, to help, to show mercy, or to open our homes in hospitality, each person and each gifting is very important in God's plan. We are to love and to value each part of the body of Christ.

We are not to compare ourselves with each other but to love one another and to pray that each of us may become all that God has called us to be.

> *For we dare not make ourselves of the number or compare ourselves with some that commend themselves: but they measuring themselves by themselves, and comparing themselves among themselves, are not wise.*
> *–2 Corinthians 10:12*

As we take heed to this, we will find that a great hindrance has been broken to becoming *"fitly joined together"* (Ephesians 4:16). As God then does His work in and through each of us, we will find that we together have become a really "good fit!" Love and respect each other. We are not all the same, but we truly need every part. Rejoice when the different parts begin to function. Each person will benefit and there is a special place for each one.

The enemy often tries to bring in spirits of jealousy and competition which destroy the effectiveness of God's people. As we resist the enemy's lies, his divisive plans are defeated as we in humility rejoice in what God is doing in each person. We need each part—they are not a threat, they are a blessing. Defeat the plans of the enemy by encouraging one another and by speaking words of life and blessing over the ministries that God is bringing forth. Always give God the glory and receive the blessing.

Each ministry is God's gift to us. He sometimes comes in strange packages, like a baby in a manger long ago, or through our brothers and our sisters who are in various stages of spiritual growth. But praise God—He comes! May we learn from the mistakes of the Pharisees, who in the time of Jesus, rejected Jesus because the package was not what they expected. May we rather rejoice that He has come and that He is moving in and through His body.

We are all called to build God's Kingdom, not our own. He is and will continue to use His many-membered body to do this. As the anointing begins to flow through the body, the day of "one man shows" will come to an end. The body of Christ will arise in the power and glory of God. We will see revival! The world again will be turned *upside down* as God comes forth in His people (see Acts 17:6b).

THIRTEEN

OPEN SHARING: PURPOSE AND GUIDELINES

The person leading the time of sharing should be prepared to encourage, teach and make room for the people to participate as God leads. If the people are new to open meetings, it is good that the leader give some guidelines along with the encouragement to share. The people need to know that the purpose of sharing is to glorify God and to edify the body.

Information regarding the protocol of open meetings is also important. We have found from experience that people ministering by turns works best. This way each person gets to share. It is not for back and forth conversation, for gossip, for sharing all our problems or to see who can perform the longest. It is not about the best song, or the longest or best testimony. Jesus is to be lifted up and our sharing should not be too lengthy but should be power packed and to the point. If we are given a teaching or a sermon that is lengthy, we need to talk to the leader ahead of time so he or she can pray into when or how it should be shared.

If controversial issues arise or questions for discussion arise, we have found that it is best to discuss these after the meeting or to set aside a time for a discussion meeting. Otherwise the meeting can easily be sidetracked. Again the purpose for open sharing is to glorify God and edify the body of Christ. In Romans 15:6, we read:

> *That ye with one mind and one mouth may glorify God, even the Father of our Lord Jesus Christ*
>
> *–Romans 15:6*

Furthermore we read in First Corinthian's the following instructions:

> *…when ye all come together … let all things be done unto edifying.*
>
> *–1 Corinthians 14 - 26*

To edify means to: build up, strengthen and to confirm.

It bears repeating that testimony time and sharing time is not a time to complain or have the "moanies"; it is a time to really show that Jesus is the answer. God is faithful and will help bring us through no matter what the circumstances are.

The goal of body ministry is to glorify God and to edify others as we minister that which has been given by the Holy Spirit. In order to be effective we want people's eyes to be upon the Lord and what He can do rather than to be looking at us for what we can do. Jesus taught in John 7:18, "*He that speaketh of himself seeketh his own glory…*" This helps us understand why our emphasis should not be on ourselves. Compared to the Lord, we can do so very little. Rather our focus should be on Jesus and His glory because that alone glorifies God and edifies others resulting in changed lives for time and eternity. When we testify about what Jesus has done in our lives, the focus is on Him for our testimony is Jesus. If it is just on self, it will not edify others or glorify God. If it is on Jesus, it will emphasize Jesus and His work in us. He has said in His Word:

> *And I, if I be lifted up from the earth, will draw all men unto me.*
> *—John 12:32*

We have the privilege of doing this each time we minister! What a mighty God!

FOURTEEN

DEALING WITH ISSUES OF CORRECTION

In an open meeting people need to be encouraged to share what God is giving them and to receive the Word He is saying to them. However, it is important to remember that people are in the process of growing and learning. Difficulty often arises when people are not aware of what God is saying or wanting to do. Sometimes the flesh or the enemy tries to take over and, as people are learning, sometimes mistakes are made. Here are some basic guidelines that can help teach the people.

TEACH THE PEOPLE TO

Check Out What is Said in the Bible

The Spirit of God will not do or say anything against His Word.

> *For there are three that bear record in heaven, the Father, the Word, and the Holy Ghost: and these three are one. And there are three that*

> *bear witness in earth, the Spirit, and the water, and the blood: and these three agree in one.*
> —1 John 5:7-8

God's Spirit and His Word will always agree. He is Holy and does not lie! The words that He speaks are spirit and truth.

"Eat the Meat and Spit Out the Bones"

> *Prove all things; hold fast that which is good*
> —1 Thessalonians 5:21

Sometimes something is said which might be regarded as controversial. A big fuss does not have to be made when this is done, nor does it necessarily have to be done publicly unless people could be hurt or led astray by what was said. If this is the case, God will give the leader wisdom in dealing with the situation as shown in some of the following examples in this section. We are called to love one another and to serve one another in love (see Galatians 5:13). Oftentimes, loving the person, praying for them and asking God for a time to share together does far more than publicly "majoring on minors." As people are taught to seek God and to search the scriptures, they will also learn to distinguish what is from the Lord and what is not, whether they are the one sharing or the one receiving from others who are sharing.

Give Godly Correction in a Godly Way

Leaders are to respond in meekness and love using the Word of God when God shows to correct someone who is in error.

> *And the servant of the Lord must not strive; but be gentle to all men, apt to teach, patient, in meekness instructing those who oppose themselves...*
>
> *–2 Timothy 2:24-25a*

God may lead you to speak to the congregation with a Word of Wisdom or clarification before or after someone has shared.

Someone once got up in an open meeting and declared that Jesus was not the Son of God. In fact, they said they would give their sound system to anyone who could prove him wrong. Rather than getting all upset and angry, one of my co-workers got up and thanked him for his fine offer—then continued on sharing from the scriptures about Jesus, the Son of God, and why He came. The sharing continued and Jesus was glorified.

Correction may also be done kindly and privately, one-on-one. It is true that those whom God loves, He also corrects. We read in Proverbs:

> *My son, despise not the chastening of the Lord; neither be weary of His correction; For whom the Lord loveth he correcteth; even as a father the son in whom He delighteth.*
>
> *–Proverbs 3:11-12*

He may do this through His Word, and usually through the leader but sometimes through someone else He chooses. It is so important to do only what God directs by His Spirit. He knows what is the best way. If we all begin correcting and straightening out everyone because it needs to be done, it will not be long before there is no open meeting at all. People will be too afraid to say or do anything because a judgmental spirit has been fostered. If, however, there is an atmosphere of godly love and godly correction as God leads, people will be free to learn and grow in God. Even mistakes can be used by God to bring about growth in all concerned if hearts are right with Him.

Correction can be done in a way that truly shows the love of God and does not scare those who are still getting up the courage to share in the meeting. Often God will have His people pray and as people are before the Lord, He will show those who are in error what is or isn't of God. God will give wisdom as we seek Him and ask Him for it.

> *But let patience have her perfect work, that ye may be perfect and entire, wanting nothing. If any of you lack wisdom, let him ask of God, that giveth to all men liberally, and upbraideth not; and it shall be given him.*
> *—James 1:4-5*

Be Patient and Kind to One Another

Pray much for the leaders to have God's leading, patience and wisdom as they minister to God's people.

As a body, we also need to be patient and kind with one another. We are all learning!

> *Be ye kind to one another, tenderhearted, forgiving one another, even as God for Christ's sake hath forgiven you.*
> *—Ephesians 4:32.*

Remember Charity (Love) Covers a Multitude of Sins

To sin is to miss the mark. We are to love one another and give people time to learn and grow. In 1 Peter we read;

> *And above all things have fervent charity among yourselves: for charity shall cover the multitude of sins.*
>
> *—1 Peter 4:8.*

Correction which is given in love is much easier to receive than correction given with a critical spirit.

Guard Against Being a "Cannibal Christian":

The following scripture provides some real wisdom that can be both taught and applied regarding body ministry:

> *For, brethren, ye have been called unto liberty; only use not liberty for an occasion to the flesh, but by love serve one another.*
> *For all the law is fulfilled in one word, even in this; Thou shalt love thy neighbor as thyself.*
> *But if ye bite and devour one another, take heed that ye be not consumed one of another.*
> *This I say then, Walk in the Spirit, and ye shall not fulfill the lust of the flesh.*
>
> *—Galatians 5:13-16*

Although the Lord has set us free and has called us to walk in liberty, that liberty is given to us for specific purposes. One of the purposes is that we walk in love and serve one another. This love can be tangibly seen when, instead of fighting and criticizing and gossiping about one another, we walk in the Spirit; honoring and loving one another as Christ has instructed us to. As a body of believers we need to lay hold of this in prayer for ourselves and each other.

Understand That God's Way is the Way of Love (1 Corinthians 13)

I remember when I was first learning to minister the Word at the hall in Calgary. God was showing me the importance of standing together in unity with the leaders that God had raised up so that we might see mighty victories in the Name of the Lord. It was a wonderful message and true. However, while I was preaching, I made a big mistake. During one part of my message I had Joshua and Aaron as the two people who held up Moses' hands, however, it should have been Aaron and Hur. While it is true unity is important and so is holding up the hands of those in leadership, unfortunately there were "bones" in this sermon.

I am so thankful that no one stood up publicly to correct me — although they could have. No one laughed or looked shocked. There wasn't a line up to show me my errors after the service. Only one lady mentioned it. She was someone whom God had used at different times to speak into my life with love. She was so gracious. She truly respected what God was doing in me as He was teaching me to preach. She corrected me in a way that also left me strengthened. I was encouraged; encouraged to press in, to pray, to search out the Word more diligently and to share the wondrous Word of the Lord as God opened doors to do so. In an atmosphere of God's love and Godly correction, the young can grow and mature. As love flows the Body of Christ can develop and come forth in healing and wholeness to do the work of God.

FIFTEEN

WE ARE CALLED TO BELIEVE GOD: NOT TO LIMIT GOD

The word of God exhorts us to truly believe God for all He has spoken to us. Often there are trials of our faith to overcome before we receive all that God has said. It was the same for the Children of Israel. They wanted out of bondage. God heard their cry and brought them out.

> *Now therefore, behold, the cry of the children of Israel is come unto me: and I have also seen the oppression wherewith the Egyptians oppress them.*
> *Come now therefore, and I will send thee unto Pharaoh, that thou mayest bring forth my people the children of Israel out of Egypt.*
> *—Exodus 3:9-10*

They had to go through the wilderness in order to come into the promised land. However, God was with them. Just as God miraculously brought them out of Egypt, He was going to miraculously take them into the promised land. He had made provision for all their needs to be met. They did not believe God, however, and because of their unbelief they limited God. Thus, a journey that would have taken less than two weeks ended up taking 40 years. As much as they wanted freedom, they turned back and tempted God many times through complaining and unbelief. They also limited the Holy One of Israel.

> *How oft did they provoke him in the wilderness,*
> *and grieve him in the desert!.*
> *Yea, they turned back and tempted God, and*
> *limited the Holy One of Israel.*
> *They remembered not his hand, nor the day*
> *when he delivered them from the enemy.*
> *—Psalm 78:40-42*

However, I believe, in this hour God is raising up a people that will learn from their example and will take the limits off of God! God is going to have a people that He truly can lead and do with as He wills. There are several areas that God is teaching us not to limit Him in regards to open meetings.

Time

In our meetings we have found that allowing God to control the timing and duration of the meetings rather than letting the clock and the demands of people do so has worked best. For example, we prayed and asked the Lord what time our Sunday meeting should be held. The Lord laid on our hearts to begin our Sunday services at 2:00 p.m. and to allow them to go as long as the Spirit of God led. For us this worked well. Many of the people we work with travel and this gave them time to do so. It also did away with the time constraints of the "noon roast" and people were free to stay as long as the Holy Spirit was moving. If someone had to go early, they were free to leave.

The component parts of the meetings also were not on a schedule and this left the Holy Spirit free to orchestrate the meetings as He willed. The meetings varied in length, anywhere from three to four hours to many more. We have found that when people are hungry for God, and when God is moving and the anointing is flowing, the time is all too soon over. However, if God is *not* moving and there is no anointing one hour can be too long! When God's Spirit begins to move among His people, people get hungry for more. Often after the meetings, many of the people get together and continue fellowshipping over supper, and then go and pray together or do whatever else God lays on hearts. For many, removing the clock has been a wonderful, liberating experience. In the busyness of our modern world, it is awesome to experience God, rather than the clock, taking charge of our time.

Who God Can Use

In past times we relied only on the pastor, worship leaders or the church leadership to hear for us but truly the limits have to come off in this area. God wants to use all His children from every ethnic background, whether young or old, rich or poor, male or female.

> *There is neither Jew nor Greek, there is neither bond nor free, there is neither male nor female:*

> *for ye are all one in Christ Jesus. And if ye be Christ's, then are ye Abraham's seed, and heirs according to the promise.*
> —*Galatians 3:28-29*

> *And I will make thy seed to multiply as the stars of heaven, and I will give unto thy seed all these countries; and in thy seed shall all the nations of the earth be blessed.*
> —*Genesis 26:4*

We gain much when we learn to receive from one another and through seeking God we learn how and when He wants to use us. As people learn to seek the face of God and to get the mind of the Lord for the service, God will begin to anoint and to bring forth His plan through different people in different ways. As people individually pray and become more aware of the mind of the Lord for themselves, they will also become more enabled to flow in this. In Psalms we read

> *Behold, all the eyes of servants look unto the hand of their masters … so our eyes wait upon the Lord our God.…*
> —*Psalms 123:2*

Does not a servant look to the hand of the master for direction? So it is with us. We wait on Him. A servant who is waiting on His master is not more or less a servant than the one who is doing what he has been commanded to do. So it is with God's people. It is the willing, obedient heart God looks for, not just the "outward performance" of what is being done. Academic ability or having a great personality is not the criteria for successful ministry. Prayerful obedience to the Lord is!

> *Not everyone that saith unto me, Lord, Lord, shall enter into the kingdom of heaven; but he that doeth the will of my Father which is in heaven.*
> *Many will say to me in that day, Lord, Lord, have we not prophesied in thy name? and in thy name have cast out devils? and in thy name done many wonderful works?*
> *And then will I profess unto them, I never knew you: depart from me, ye that work iniquity.*
> *–Matthew 7:21-23*

If God wants to use us to speak, or use us to pray for the one(s) speaking, we need to know that both praying or speaking are equally important and both are to be valued. If we are the one God uses to pray the prayer of faith for healing and miracles, or if He uses us to come alongside in agreement in prayer, we need to know that both are important and valuable. As people become more secure in God and learn this principle of willing obedience from the heart; jealousy, competition and insecurities will flee away. The focus will no longer be on self and performance, but upon God—His plan, His way, and His glory! Then we will rejoice in whatever way He moves and in whomever He uses, for the focus will be on Him! It is His Kingdom, not ours.

Dare to believe God for the impossible! Believe Him to break down the barriers and to bring forth His will. Let's believe God together and pray, *"Thy Kingdom come. Thy will be done in earth, as it is in heaven"* (Matthew 6:10).

As the Spirit of God has moved, we have seen people who, in the natural, would not consider themselves to be singers get up in a service under the anointing of God and sing down the Glory of God. We have seen others who had never spoken publicly get up and preach under a powerful anointing as they yielded to the Lord. I remember a young girl of just 15 years old at the hall in Calgary getting up and preaching her first sermon like she had been preaching a life-time. We have seen God take a Caucasian corporate business executive and raise him up to become a loving pastor to a primarily native assembly. We have seen Him take a shy, young married native lady with children and turn her into an anointed fiery evangelist, who preaches the Word of God in power and has the loving support of her husband.

We have had the joy of seeing God raise up preachers, prophetic and teaching ministries, as well as missionaries as they have had the freedom to come forth in God. We have seen drug addicts set free and turned into preachers who have stood true to God through the tests of time. We have seen prayer warriors arise who truly move the hand of God. We have seen children prophesying, preaching and praying for the sick as the limits have come off. God has had the freedom in various services to develop and use His people. It is He who did the work and it is He who gets the glory! What a loss it would have been if this had not happened or had not been allowed and encouraged. The choosing is of God, and not man. Let us not limit Him, but rather rejoice as the limits come off and He brings forth His people to show forth the glory of God. May He truly have His way in each of us.

Many of us have been like those who began in the Cave of Adullam. This story is found in the book of First Samuel.

> *David therefore departed thence, and escaped to the cave Adullam; and when his brethren and all his father's house heard it, they went down thither to him.*
>
> *And every one that was in distress, and everyone that was in debt, and everyone that was discontented, gathered themselves unto him; and he became a captain over them; and there were with him about four hundred men.*
>
> *—1 Samuel 22:1-2*

This small group of distressed men became known as David's Mighty Men. The Lord raised them up as mighty men of God who became victorious warriors, powerfully used by Him, to overcome the enemy against all odds.

Now, as it was then, God is bringing forth His servants and is developing and training them for His Kingdom purposes. The people of God are arising and taking their place. In so doing they are becoming a force to be reckoned with as they take the limits off God and believe Him for all He has promised.

SIXTEEN

EXPANDING VISION FOR KINGDOM PURPOSES

God so often wants to do exceedingly above all we can ask or think. Praise God! He is teaching us to take the limits off. Not only does God want to bless the local body of believers to which we belong; He wants to move upon His body everywhere and multiply it all across the land. We have seen other places where God is moving in freedom and we rejoice in what He is doing. He wants to use all His people! We limit God if our focus is inward or on our vision alone and we lose much if we become a "bless-me club." God has so much more for us. There's a lost and dying world out there and it's harvest time.

You and I are privileged to live in this hour for we get to be a part of the end-time harvest. In harvest time it's "all hands on deck!" Sometimes we don't understand what God is doing. Sometimes we are like the twelve disciples who, rather than waiting on God, all went shopping (see John 4:8). Jesus, who would only do what His Father showed Him to do, waited by the well in the heat of the day. He ministered to one woman who was used to bring a multitude to Him. His heart was for the lost! No wonder He said to His surprised disciples on their return from shopping, "*...Lift up your eyes, and look on the fields; for they are white already to harvest*" (John 4:35).

May God move our hearts with compassion for the lost as Jesus' heart was moved, whether for one soul or for the multitude (Matthew 14:14). Then waiting on God for His direction and stepping out in faith as He gives it will become so much more important than the things that so easily rob our time with Him.

DEVELOP A HEART FOR OUTREACH:

We must have a heart for outreach if we are truly to come forth in all God wants. Just as we learn to come forth in our respective ministries in the local assembly, so it is, that as we seek God, He will bring us forth in terms of reaching out to others with the life-giving Gospel of Jesus Christ. The ministries of intercession, faith, the giving of finances, helps, evangelism, hospitality, showing of mercy, healing, preaching, teaching, the prophetic and apostolic ministries, the raising up of pastors and other ministries will begin to develop and function as God brings the people forth.

These ministries are birthed by the Spirit as people seek God in prayer and in the Word and begin to function as God leads in the assembly. They are not promoted or elected by man, but developed and anointed by God. As the people come forth in the local assembly many will, if encouraged and released to do so, begin to flow out into the streets, the schools, local businesses and other places as God leads. We need to release them and to help them to build God's Kingdom as God directs.

The local assembly was never meant to just be a container to store Christians in. It is to be a place where people are sent forth to minister and a place where they can also return to, to be refreshed, refilled and sent out again as the Holy Spirit leads. Examples of this can be seen in the book of Acts.

> *Now there were in the church that was at Antioch certain prophets and teachers; as Barnabas, and Simeon that was called Niger, and Lucius of Cyrene, and Manaen, which had been brought up with Herod the tetrarch, and Saul.*
> *As they ministered to the Lord, and fasted, the Holy Ghost said, Separate me Barnabas and Saul for the work whereunto I have called them.*
> *And when they had fasted and prayed, and laid their hands on them, they sent them away.*
> *So they, being sent forth by the Holy Ghost, departed unto Seleucia; and from thence they sailed to Cyprus.*
> —Acts 13:1-4

Two other examples of this can be seen in the following scriptures; Acts 4:23-31 and Acts 15:25-35.

Not only does God want to use us personally, but we also get to be a part of what God is doing as we encourage and help others to come forth in ministry. This is truly exciting, for what God births in each person is His gift to us if we will receive from that gift and cherish it as from Him. As well, in blessing and encouraging what God is doing in and through others as He sends them out, we also participate and rejoice in the harvest they reap as more souls are brought into our Father's Kingdom.

Our Attitude Regarding Other Groups

This concept of blessing others extends to other groups that God is using for His purposes as well. May we also pray for and rejoice as we hear of the good things that God is doing in and through our brothers and sisters in groups that are different from us. We are all part of His body if we are born again. God is not divided against Himself, so we as His people are learning not to be divided either. Just as an eye, a heart, a mouth and feet are important parts of the body, so it is with us. Each one of us is needed and is responsible to be where God has led us to be. As we walk in that freedom and release others to do the same, we can bless one another and no longer limit or hinder what God would do through His many-membered body.

Praise God, the spirits of competition, pride, jealousy, division and sectarianism are coming down and are being defeated in and through God's people. As we come into unity with the purposes and the will of God, we will see His blessing come forth in awesome ways (see Psalm 133). It is only as we are chosen and ordained of God and are in submission to Him, that we can walk in His authority and see His Kingdom purposes accomplished. It is God who decides what gifts and ministries are needful in His body and it is He who places them in the various members of the body as He pleases.

Thank God that we each have the privilege of being part of what God is doing. As we prepare our hearts for a mighty visitation of God across the land, let us rejoice and pray for one another and give God the glory for what He is doing.

SEVENTEEN

GODLY LEADERSHIP

Although group participation under the direction of the Holy Spirit is encouraged and valued in open meetings, God still has those whom He has called and appointed to lead. These leaders are to be chosen and ordained by God, not only by man. A model of this process can be seen in Mark chapter 3.

> *And he goeth up into a mountain, and calleth unto Himself whom He would: and they came unto Him.*
> *And He ordained twelve, that they should be with Him, that He might send them forth to preach,*
> *And to have power to heal sicknesses, and to cast out devils.*
> *—Mark 3:13-15*

When Jesus walked on earth there was a multitude of people who heard Him preach. From the multitudes, there were men and women who really decided to follow Him. From those that were following Him, Jesus chose to ordain twelve as leaders. They were ordained that first of all they should be with Him and then, from the place of His presence, He would send them forth to preach, to heal the sick and to cast out devils. They would go forth and do the works of God in response to Jesus sending them and this way they went forth totally under His authority with heaven backing them.

These disciples were raised up into leadership from the place of following after Jesus with all their hearts. They were not perfect, but the hand of God was upon them. So it is today. There are those who are truly following Jesus with all their hearts and out of these, God has and will continue to raise up those whom He ordains to become leaders amongst His people. The success of their ministry will depend on whether or not their lives continue to be committed to being with Jesus, and that as they are sent out to do His works, they stay under His authority and walk in obedience to Him.

> *And He gave some, apostles; and some prophets; and some, evangelists; and some, pastors and teachers; For the perfecting of the saints, for the work of the ministry, for the edifying of the body of Christ.*
> *—Ephesians 4:11.12*

> *But now hath God set the members every one of them in the body, as it hath pleased Him.*
> *—I Cor. 12:18*

These leaders do not function because of election, politics or the will of man, but by the anointing, appointment and authority of the Holy Spirit. It is God who raises these leaders up. As the people look to the Lord, they will usually recognize when God is doing this (see Acts 4:13). For example, in our assembly, God raised up a pastor from the congregation. The leaders encouraged him and gave him opportunity to develop his ministry and they rejoiced in God's choice for pastor for the assembly. Most of the congregation recognized by the Spirit of God that this was happening; they began to receive him as such before he himself was willing to take his place or to confirm that he knew God had truly called him in this way. When he did, there was great joy and the people were a wonderful part of his ordination. Those who had been leading stepped back as he took his place and they went on to minister in other areas that God had called them to. After he had pastored, for approximately ten years, he retired but by that time, the Lord had already raised up another pastor and an assistant for the assembly. As God has led, the leader who began the work and the leaders who were there throughout the early years of the assembly's establishment, return periodically to teach, preach and support and encourage the pastors and the assembly in the work of the Lord.

In retrospect, it is wonderful to see how God has worked. There was no striving or jealousy—God confirmed many times to all concerned who God's choices were to pastor the work. God raised these pastors up from within the assembly, ordained, appointed and anointed them, and we all have rejoiced in what God has done!

In Proverbs 18:16 we read, *"A man's gift makes room for him and bringeth him before great men."* This is surely true in the spiritual realm. To be used by God people do not have to strive or use political means. God makes the way as we, in humility, walk in His ways. In Psalms we read:

> *Lift not your horn* [or power] *on high: Speak not with a stiff* [proud] *neck. For promotion cometh neither from the east, nor from the west, not from the south. But God is the judge: He putteth one down and setteth up another*
> —Psalm 75:5-7 [insertions by author]

True promotion does not come from man, it comes from God! As God's will is sought by all concerned, God will show and will bring forth His leaders. God's will, not a particular position, is to be sought. As the meetings continue many leaders will be raised up and the group will be blessed as God's plans and purposes are brought forth.

Godly leaders are to be cherished. They are to feed the flock, to care for their souls and to be godly examples to the people.

> *Feed the flock of God which is among you, taking the oversight thereof, not by constraint, but willingly; not for filthy lucre, but of a ready mind; Neither as being lords over God's heritage, but being examples to the flock.*
> —1 Peter 5:2-3

> *Obey them that have the rule over you, and submit yourselves: for they watch for your souls, as they that must give account, that they may do it with joy, and not with grief: for that is unprofitable for you.*
> —Hebrews 13:17

Leadership is a calling not a 9 to 5 job. Leaders are to truly love the people. This love also needs to be expressed in practical ways, such as really listening to people and by helping, visiting and praying with them as God directs. Like Jesus, the Chief Shepherd, godly leaders are to help facilitate the fullness of God's plan to come forth in each life as God leads. I thank God for godly leaders who have spoken into my life. Even as Jesus was with His disciples, so godly leaders are to follow His example concerning those God entrusts into their care.

I remember when, as a new minister, I was invited by an experienced, Spirit-led minister and his wife, to help lead a ministry team on an outreach to Trinidad. What a time of incredible growth it was for me personally. I learned and experienced much during that time. We saw God move in wonderful ways. Today we also take other young people with us on our own summer outreaches as part of our NTOMI discipleship training team. Some of them are coming forth in ministry and will also mentor and speak into the lives of others.

Jesus worked with the disciples to see them become able ministers. He took time with them, taught them and encouraged them to minister. He gave them room to learn and the opportunity to come forth in ministry. He helped the disciples develop because He knew He would not always be with them. Jesus desired that they fully become the ministers God had called them to be. He taught them that they should go and also make disciples and see them raised up. As we read in the book of Matthew, Jesus told His disciples:

> *...I have been given all authority in heaven and on earth. Therefore, go and make disciples of all nations, baptizing them in the name of the Father and the Son and the Holy Spirit.*

> *Teach these new disciples to obey all the commands I have given you. And be sure of this: I am with you always, even to the end of the age.*
>
> —Matthew 28:18-20 (NLT)[3]

This is how the Gospel spreads and it spreads in power! He also encouraged them saying:

> *Verily, verily, I say unto you, He that believeth on me, the works that I do shall he do also; and greater works than these shall he do; because I go unto my Father.*
>
> —John 14:12

Paul caught it and taught it as can be seen in his instructions to his spiritual son Timothy. In second Timothy we read:

> *And the things that thou hast heard of me among many witnesses, the same commit thou to faithful men, who shall be able to teach others also.*
>
> —2 Timothy 2:20

It is also very important that the leaders commit to taking time to seek and to wait on God for His order to come forth in the meetings, as well as for the Word of the Lord for each particular meeting. It is essential for leaders never to trust in natural ability alone but always to seek God for the anointing to deliver that which God will give to them in the secret place of prayer. They are to make sure the flock is fed. They are, with God's grace and help,

---

3   Matthew 29:18-20 (NLT)

to be a good example. Much of the instruction applies to leadership today which Paul gave to Timothy,

> *Let no man despise thy youth; but be thou an example of the believers, in word, in conversation, in charity, in spirit, in faith, in purity.*
> *Till I come, give attendance to reading, to exhortation, to doctrine.*
> *Neglect not the gift that is in thee, which was given thee by prophecy, with the laying on of the hands of the presbytery.*
> *Meditate upon these things; give thyself wholly to them; that thy profiting may appear to all.*
> *Take heed unto thyself, and unto the doctrine; continue in them: for in doing this thou shalt both save thyself, and them that hear thee.*
> —1 Timothy 4:12-16

Leaders must be prepared to minister the Word of God in season and sometimes out of season. Even if someone else is to preach, they need to ask God to help them stand in the gap if necessary. I remember in one of our meetings how God had been anointing a particular person as she would share the Word. She would usually speak for five to ten minutes and it was good. I asked her if she would prepare to preach the following Sunday and she said, "*yes!*" That Sunday, she began to preach and after five minutes said, "*I can't*" and promptly sat down. By the grace and power of God, the Word of the Lord rose up in me and God gave me the rest of the message. Truly our dependence is on Him and He gets the glory.

The leader of the meeting often functions like a Holy Ghost-led "emcee." As the leader waits on the Lord and is sensitive to Him, God will begin to show the leader His will throughout the meeting. God may show them to keep singing a particular song because God is going to move, or to wait in His presence because someone is going to prophesy. He may give them a word of encouragement or exhortation when the meeting is tight and will show them what to do in various situations. Often times God's leading will come as He speaks to the leader through His still small voice. At other times God will move as well through others, thus confirming His will for the meeting. However, each time God speaks it requires a step of faith to move out in obedience and, as for many who are in the public eye, this is not always easy to do. This is one of the reasons why, for some, it is easier to slip back into man's order rather than to take the risk and continue to move out in faith throughout each service, endeavoring to hear and obey the Lord for the fullness of His plan alone. Truly "we have not been this way before" and we need God! Not only do the leaders need to pray but we also need to pray for the leaders. May God help each leader and encourage them as they continue to seek God's direction to lead the meetings and to boldly walk in obedience to Him rather than to fall back into the ways of man.

EIGHTEEN

FINANCES AND INTEGRITY

If you are led to receive offerings in your group, you need to know that the handling of finances in the group is a very important issue. Finances are an area where greed, undue pressure, as well as ungodly uses of money collected has caused many to stumble. We must be accountable for the finances that are received. Integrity in anything to do with the receiving or the use of offerings is key, as is integrity in every area of life and ministry. We are to be godly examples in character and in our actions. As we look to the Lord, He will help us.

There are several things we have learned that are helpful concerning finances. We have found it is not wise to look to man to supply what only God can supply. We also have found that God is faithful. Hudson Taylor, founder of China Inland Mission, once said that *"God's work, done God's way will never lack God's supply."*[4]

People need to know it is scriptural to give; however, we are never to beg and manipulate. If God so leads, an offering plate can be passed around or a container can be

---

4 Hudson Taylor, quoted in video entitled "Hudson Taylor (Ken Anderson Films,1989)

put out for people to give as they feel led. The scriptures teach us:

> *...He which soweth sparingly shall reap also sparingly; and he with soweth bountifully shall reap also bountifully.*
> *Every man according as he purposeth in his heart, so let him give; not grudgingly, or of necessity: for God loveth a cheerful giver.*
> *And God is able to make all grace abound toward you; that ye, always having all sufficiency in all things, may abound to every good work.*
> *–2 Corinthians 9: 6-8*

We are to go to God to meet our needs. He is our supply and He is faithful. Focus on Him and His provision rather than on the need at hand. He will supply what is needed to accomplish His plans as we look to Him. In Philippians 4:19 we read, *"But my God shall supply all your need according to His riches in glory by Christ Jesus."* As we look to Him alone, we will find that truly He will not fail to see His plans and purposes accomplished.

We have found praying and going to God rather than man is so vital even during the times that our faith has been greatly tested regarding these matters. We are truly thankful for the miracles we have seen in this area. Over and over again we have been able to testify of the faithfulness of our awesome God.

As has been already said, it is crucial that the finances be handled with integrity and accountability. If finances start coming in on a regular basis, a system of accountability must be set in place. Finances which are given for the meetings are to be used for meeting expenses not for personal gain.

The keeping of accurate records shows where and how the finances have been used. Financial records should be kept of all income which has been received. This should include the person's name, address, and the amount given. As well, all outgoing expenses should be recorded and receipts for these expenses should be kept along with the financial records. Someone familiar with accounting or bookkeeping can help you get set up correctly so that you will be able to maintain accurate records. It is most highly recommended that you consult with someone who can help you with this.

We have also been asked if income tax receipts can be given out by groups which have become a local assembly in their community. This can only be done as they form a legal board and meet the requirements of Revenue Canada to obtain charitable status and a charitable tax number. More information can be obtained through Revenue Canada concerning this. (Those residing outside of Canada can contact the appropriate government agencies for their country.)

Pray and ask God how to be good stewards of the resources God brings in. We believe that at least 10% of what comes in should go into other ministries. Sow richly into the harvest fields of the Lord. Never grow inward with finances, but rather let God bless others through you as you keep your vision high. Let God give you His vision for outreach. Be blessed as you bless because God created us not only to receive His blessings, but also to be a blessing to many, to be fruitful and to multiply. Whether it is in giving finances, prayer, or in the giving of our lives, we cannot out give God!

NINETEEN

PREPARING FOR GOOD MEETINGS

Anything worth doing is worth doing well and to do things well requires preparation. Whether you are an Olympic racer, a chef planning a banquet, a preacher planning a sermon or someone participating in an open meeting, preparation is of paramount importance. Without preparation, skills are not developed fully, things are forgotten or left out and what is being done often leaves much to be desired. Yes, as we prepare with all our hearts to do what God has asked, we have the joy of knowing we have given Him our very best.

> *And whatsoever ye do, do it heartily, as to the Lord, and not unto men. Knowing that of the Lord ye shall receive the reward of the inheritance: for ye serve the Lord Christ.*
> —Colossians 3:23-24

KEYS TO A GOOD MEETING

In open meetings many people share. It is so important for each person to learn to take responsibility to prepare for a good meeting. We are to give our best and in order to do this we need God's anointing and help. We are dependent on Him to do the work by his Holy Spirit. It is key that we learn to wait upon the Lord during the week and to prepare our hearts for Him to move.

There are several keys that are helpful to remember in terms of preparation.

It is key to:

Prepare in Prayer

Meeting together is not a spectator sport; we all need to be before the Lord in prayer for His will to come forth. As we "prepare in prayer" God's anointing begins to come and God will move in people to bring forth His plan and His order for the meeting. We need our hearts to be prepared in prayer and to be ready and available for what God would have. Jesus teaches us in Matthew:

> *But thou, when thou prayest, enter into thy closet, and when thou has shut thy door, pray to thy Father which is in secret; and thy Father which seeth in secret shall reward thee openly.*
> —Matthew 6:6

Ask Him what He wants you to do. As we separate ourselves unto the Lord in the secret place, God will often place within our hearts a desire for fresh consecration. It is in this place that we are transformed and prepared by God for His will. In Romans, the Apostle Paul exhorts believers with the following words:

> *I beseech you therefore, brethren, by the mercies of God, that ye present your bodies a living sacrifice, holy, acceptable unto God, which is*

> *your reasonable service And be not conformed to this world: but be ye transformed by the renewing of your mind, that ye may prove what is that good, and acceptable, and perfect will of God.*
>
> *—Romans 12:1-2*

God wants to meet with us and have us walk according to His will in every area of our lives. It is so important when we minister, that we minister according to the will of God. This is what God will bless and this will bring forth precious fruit in His Kingdom. Whether it is in our daily life or in our times of ministry and service, may we truly be led by the Spirit of God (see Romans 8:14).

Wait on Your Ministry

In the book of Romans we read:

> *For as we have many members in one body, and all members have not the same office:*
> *So we, being many, are one body in Christ, and every one members one of another.*
> *Having then gifts differing according to the grace that is given to us, whether prophecy, let us prophesy according to the proportion of faith;*
> *Or ministry, let us wait on our ministering: or he that teacheth, on teaching;*
> *Or he that exhorteth, on exhortation: he that giveth, let him do it with simplicity; he that ruleth, with diligence; he that sheweth mercy, with cheerfulness.*
>
> *—Romans 12: 4-8*

Give yourself completely to God and to His purposes as part of the many membered body of Christ. Wait upon Him; let Him develop your character as well as your gifting and ministry. As you wait upon the Lord in prayer He will begin to lead you and teach you concerning ministry. He will also anoint you to come forth in terms of your ministry gifting as you spend time with Him.

As we seek the Lord, He gives us the grace and ability to stand in the face of persecution or in times of difficult circumstances. Often God shows that what we preach and minister is true by our ability to stand in difficult times. It is in these times the people see the reality of God in our lives. As people see our faith in action, we earn the right to be heard. Become rooted and grounded in His love and in His Word as you;

> *Study to shew thyself approved unto God, a workman that needeth not to be ashamed, rightly dividing the word of truth.*
> *—2 Timothy 2:15*

Be Good Stewards of What God Has Given You

In God's Word we are exhorted:

> *As every man hath received the gift, even so minister the same one to another as good stewards of the manifold grace of God.*
> *If any man speak, let him speak as the oracles of God; if any man minister, let him do it with the ability which God giveth; that God in all things may be glorified through Jesus Christ,*

> *to whom be praise and dominion forever and ever. Amen*
>
> *—1 Peter 4:10-11*

We are to minister that which God gives us to minister, as God leads. Again, the purpose of this is, that God be glorified (see 1 Peter 4:11), that the body be edified and that His will be done.

> *And he gave some, apostles; and some, prophets; and some, evangelists; and some, pastors and teachers;*
> *For the perfecting of the saints, for the work of the ministry, for the edifying of the body of Christ:*
> *Till we all come in the unity of the faith, and of the knowledge of the Son of God, unto a perfect man, unto the measure of the stature of the fulness of Christ:*
> *That we henceforth be no more children, tossed to and fro, and carried about with every wind of doctrine, by the sleight of men, and cunning craftiness, whereby they lie in wait to deceive;*
> *But speaking the truth in love, may grow up into him in all things, which is the head, even Christ:*
> *From whom the whole body fitly joined together and compacted by that which every joint supplieth, according to the effectual working in the measure of every part, maketh increase of the body unto the edifying of itself in love.*
>
> *—Ephesians 4:11-16*

We ask God for the boldness and the sensitivity to Him and to His timing to enable us to do this. As each one freely receives and freely gives what God has given, under God's direction, a good meeting truly will be experienced.

Love One Another

When Jesus was teaching His disciples and preparing them for ministry, He told them that they were to love one another even as He loved them. This kind of love between them, He said, would show the world that they were truly His disciples.

> *A new commandment I give unto you, That ye love one another; as I have loved you, that ye also love one another.*
> *By this shall all men know that ye are my disciples, if ye have love one to another.*
> *—John 13:34-35*

The more we walk in God's love, the more people are drawn to Him. Whether it is in our meetings or in our everyday life, the love of Jesus flowing through His many membered body will draw others to Him. It also gives credibility to the reality of the Gospel we preach.

We are further exhorted in Peter:

> *Above all things have intense and unfailing love for one another, for love covers a multitude of sins* [forgives and disregards the offenses of others].
> *—1 Peter 4:8 AMP[5]*

---

5   I Peter 4:8 (AMP)

It is this kind of love Jesus has for us and we are to have one for another. It is this kind of love that endures the trials of life and the test of time.

Speak Words of Life

It is so important as believers, we learn to speak words of life.

> *A brother offended is harder to be won than a strong city: and their contentions are like the bars of a castle.*
> *A man's belly shall be satisfied with the fruit of his mouth; and with the increase of his lips shall he be filled.*
> *Death and life are in the power of the tongue: and they that love it shall eat the fruit thereof.*
> *—Proverbs 18:19-21*

The enemy accuses, puts down and loves it when people or groups get offended or speak words of death. When these things happen, we are not to be like Satan and use words of accusation. Jesus teaches us to intercede in prayer instead of agreeing with the accuser of the brethren. As we intercede in faith, words of life and empowerment are released.

We read in Proverbs 18:21a, *"Death and life are in the power of the tongue..."* According to Strong's Concordance[6], the word *power* comes from the Hebrew word *"hand" (the open one—indicating power, means, direction,*

---

[6] James Strong, Strong's Exhaustive Concordance of the Bible – Together with:
Dictionaries of the Hebrew and Greek Words (Peabody, MA: Hendrickson Publishers, ISBN 0-917006-01-1) Hebrew Dictionary,

etc.). Our words either release the hand of life or death upon ourselves and others. God's people are to be like Jesus who spoke and ministered words of life and blessing. In John 6:63b we read the words of Jesus as He shared … *"the words that I speak unto you, are spirit, and they are life."* We, God's people are to speak the truth in love and humility instead of speaking words of death and accusation. We need to ask God to help us in this area. He will give us the wisdom, the godly love and the help we need to truly speak words of life and blessing.

As King David of old, may we also pray the prayer found in Psalm;

> *Let the words of my mouth, and the meditation of my heart, be acceptable in thy sight, O Lord, my strength, and my redeemer.*
>
> *–Psalm 19:14*

When God does the work in our hearts, our mouths will be filled with good things. We will be a people who praise and glorify God and see Him move in wonderful ways. David found this to be so as he wrote in Psalm 50;

> *Whoso offereth praise glorifieth me: to him that ordereth his conversation aright will I show the salvation of God.*
>
> *–Psalm 50:23*

According to the Strong's Concordance[7], the word *salvation* in Psalm 50:23 comes from the Hebrew word meaning *"liberty, deliverance, prosperity."* Is this not what we want in our own personal lives, our meetings, our ministry and also for the people that we minister to?

---

7   Ibid.

Truly, we serve an awesome God who wants to move in and through His people. As we allow Him to do the work in us we will see Him come forth in power in all areas of our lives and ministries and we will prosper in the things of the Lord.

Pray and Obey

When we, God's people, "pray and obey," we shall see God move in awesome ways. The prophet Jeremiah knew this. In Jeremiah 33:3, we read how God's people are instructed by God to call upon Him and God will answer them and show them wonderful things which they didn't know. God begins to show us His plan as we pray. As we continue in prayer and obey that which He asks us to do, His plan comes to pass. How wonderful it is that God would give us His plan for the meeting or for anything else! We know that God will bless His plan but unfortunately, so often people come up with their own plans and just ask God to bless them. We need to lay hold of the plan of God in prayer because that is the plan that will be blessed and that's the plan that will work.

James gives us the following admonition;

> *But be ye doers of the word, and not hearers only, deceiving your own selves.*
> *–James 1:22*

As God gives us His plan and His instructions, we truly need to walk in obedience if we are going to see His works done in our lives and in our meetings.

In Matthew, Jesus instructs us saying:

> *Not everyone who says to Me, Lord, Lord, will enter the kingdom of heaven, but he who does the will of my Father who is heaven.*
> *Many will say to Me on that day, Lord, Lord, have we not prophesied in Your name and driven out demons in Your name and done many mighty works in Your name?*
> *And then I will say to them openly* [publicly], *I never knew you; depart from Me, you who act wickedly* [disregarding My commands].
> –Matthew 7:21-23 AMP[8]

It is absolutely crucial that we pray and obey. As we pray, God will make His will known. Through prayer, God shows His ways and as He alone holds the keys to the hearts of men, He knows what will turn their hearts unto Him.

No wonder Jesus teaches us the importance of obedience. Jesus taught that those who hear His Word and do it are like a man who builds his house upon the rock. That house withstands the storms of time. He also taught that those who hear His Word and do not do it, are like a man who built his house on sand. When the storms of life come, that house falls (see Matthew 7:24-27).

We are called to build the house of the Lord. That which we build will stand the test of time as we walk in obedience to God and build upon the rock Christ Jesus. God's Word also says, "*The willing and the obedient shall eat the good of the land*" (Isaiah 1:19).

---

[8] Matthew 7:21-23 (AMP)

This willingness and obedience is what the Spirit of the Lord is calling us to. As we walk in obedience to God and to the things that He shows in the place of prayer, we will be amazed at what the Lord will do in and through His people. Even as David's army did not stay in the cave of Adullam or continue in the state in which they began, so shall it be for God's people.

> *... every one that was in distress, and everyone that was in debt, and everyone that was discontented, gathered themselves unto him; and he became a captain over them: and there were with him about four hundred men.*
> *−1 Samuel 22:1-2*

Later we read that David's army, with its lowly beginnings, had multiplied by thousands of men. In fact, Gill's Commentary[9] states, that there were upwards of 348,800 men who joined themselves to David at Hebron. God had done an awesome work!

> *All these men of war, that could keep rank, came with a perfect heart to Hebron, to make David king over all Israel: and all the rest also of Israel were of one heart to make David king.*
> *−1 Chronicles 12:38*

Like King David's army of old, God's people shall come out of the "caves" of obscurity where they have been hidden away, learning from the Living God (see 1 Chronicles 11:9-12:38). They shall come forth changed into His likeness and image, an exceedingly great and experienced "army," vibrant and alive in the Spirit of God,

---

9   Gill's Exposition of the Entire Bible, Biblehub.com

strong in the Lord and the power of His Might, doing exploits and fulfilling God's Word in the Name of the Lord. They will proclaim Jesus Christ, King of Kings and Lord of Lords, throughout the land.

CONCLUSION

God is raising up a people. One of the ways He is moving and teaching His people is through open meetings and body ministry. For those that God is calling in this way, open meetings can truly be a blessing as His people are encouraged to seek God and to come forth in Him. When they are trained up in open meetings and become experienced in responding to, and moving out in the things of God, we will see a people rise up in God who will be able to effectively minister as the end time harvest of the earth comes in.

If we, His people submit ourselves fully to the will and the Spirit of Almighty God, we will walk in His authority both individually and corporately and we again will know the day of His visitation. The presence of the Lord shall be known in power and it will flow out afresh like a mighty river from the House of the Lord to a lost and dying world. As Jesus is exalted and lifted high, He will draw men unto Himself and we, His people:

> ... *Shall know, if we follow on to know the Lord: His going forth is prepared as the morning: and He shall come unto us as the rain, as the latter and the former rain unto the earth.*
>
> *–Hosea 6:3*

May the Lord truly bless, anoint, empower and use you as you follow on to know Him for:

> *...Those who know their God will be strong and do exploits.*
>
> *–Daniel 11:32b*

May you see the fullness of His mighty plan fulfilled in your life; for each of us as His children—dearly loved by Him—have been called to minister in Jesus Name.

There is a place deep within each of us that only the moving's of the Spirit of God can satisfy. Jesus spoke about this in the Book of John:

> *...if any man thirst, let him come unto me, and drink. He that believeth on me, as the scripture hath said, out of his belly shall flow rivers of living water.*
>
> *–John 7: 37b-38*

May we, His people, come unto Him and drink deeply, believing on Him as the scriptures have said and may we truly receive of His Spirit and let the rivers flow!

FOOT NOTES AND CREDITS

1 Special Note

2 Crossway.Org This Day in History: Jonathan Edwards Preaches "Sinners in the Hands of an Angry God"

3 Matthew 29:18-20 (NLT)

4 Hudson Taylor, quoted in filed entitled "Hudson Taylor (Ken Anderson Films,1989)

5 I Peter 4:8 (AMP)

6 James Strong, Strong's Exhaustive Concordance of the Bible – Together with:

Dictionaries of the Hebrew and Greek Words (Peabody, MA: Hendrickson Publishers, ISBN 0-917006-01-1) Hebrew Dictionary,

7 Ibid.,

8 Matthew 7:21-23 (AMP)

9 Gill's Exposition of the Entire Bible, Biblehub.com

Appendix A

10 AllAboutGod.com - The Body of Christ

Appendix A

AllAboutGod.com

The Body Of Christ

Definition

> *"The Body of Christ is a common, yet complex term used in the Christian faith. Some may initially think we are talking about the physical body of Christ, as in His human form on earth. But the term "Body of Christ" actually refers to the members of His church, throughout history. Who or what is the body of Christ? The body of Christ is the Church, made up of all those who have accepted Jesus Christ as their personal Savior. Each Christian, then, is a part of the body of Christ."*[10]

Two of the main scriptural references to the body of Christ are found in the book of 1st Corinthians 12 and in the book of Ephesians 4.

These Scriptures show in a very beautiful way how the parts of the body of Christ are to work together and why it works together to see the purposes of God fulfilled.

---

[10] Definition published by All about God.com

1 Corinthians 12:12-27

12** For as the body is one, and hath many members, and all the members of that one body, being many, are one body: so also is Christ. **13** For by one Spirit are we all baptized into one body, whether we be Jews or Gentiles, whether we be bond or free; and have been all made to drink into one Spirit. **14** For the body is not one member, but many. **15** If the foot shall say, Because I am not the hand, I am not of the body; is it therefore not of the body? **16** And if the ear shall say, Because I am not the eye, I am not of the body; is it therefore not of the body? **17** If the whole body were an eye, where were the hearing? If the whole were hearing, where were the smelling? **18** But now hath God set the members every one of them in the body, as it hath pleased him. **19** And if they were all one member, where were the body? **20** But now are they many members, yet but one body. **21** And the eye cannot say unto the hand, I have no need of thee: nor again the head to the feet, I have no need of you. **22** Nay, much more those members of the body, which seem to be more feeble, are necessary: **23** And those members of the body, which we think to be less honourable, upon these we bestow more abundant honour; and our uncomely parts have more abundant comeliness. **24** For our comely parts have no need: but God hath tempered the body together, having given more abundant honour to that part which lacked: **25** That* *there should be no schism in the body; but that the members should have the same care one for another.* ***26 *And whether one member suffer, all the members suffer with it; or one member be honoured, all the members rejoice with it.*

27 *Now ye are the body of Christ, and members in particular.*

Ephesians 4:11-16

11 *And he gave some, apostles; and some, prophets; and some, evangelists; and some, pastors and teachers;* ***12*** *For the perfecting of the saints, for the work of the ministry, for the edifying of the body of Christ:* ***13*** *Till we all come in the unity of the faith, and of the knowledge of the Son of God, unto a perfect man, unto the measure of the stature of the fulness of Christ:* ***14*** *That we henceforth be no more children, tossed to and fro, and carried about with every wind of doctrine, by the sleight of men, and cunning craftiness, whereby they lie in wait to deceive;* ***15*** *But speaking the truth in love, may grow up into him in all things, which is the head, even Christ:* ***16*** *From whom the whole body fitly joined together and compacted by that which every joint supplieth, according to the effectual working in the measure of every part, maketh increase of the body unto the edifying of itself in love.*

As we, the body of Christ learn to function consistently as a strong, healthy body, we will find that we walk consistently under the commanded blessing of God, *"even life forever more"* [Psalms 133]. Again the world will be able to say, *"behold how they love one another"*, as the church fulfils the commands given in John chapters 14 and 15. As we learn to love one another as Christ has loved us we will see the works of God come forth in our lives and the lives that we are called to minister in Jesus name.

To order more copies of this book, find books by other
Canadian authors, or make inquiries about publishing
your own book, contact PageMaster at:

PageMaster Publication Services Inc.
11340-120 Street, Edmonton, AB T5G 0W5
books@pagemaster.ca
780-425-9303

catalogue and e-commerce store
PageMasterPublishing.ca/Shop

www.ingramcontent.com/pod-product-compliance
Lightning Source LLC
Chambersburg PA
CBHW061446040426
42450CB00007B/1234